Sabbath in the City
Sustaining Urban Pastoral Excellence

Bryan P. Stone and Claire E. Wolfteich

Westminster John Knox Press
LOUISVILLE • LONDON

Scripture quotations, unless otherwise indicated, are from the New Revised Standard Version of the Bible, copyright © 1989 by the Division of Christian Education of the National Council of the Churches of Christ in the U.S.A., and are used by permission.

Excerpt from *A Timbered Choir* is copyright © 1999 by Wendell Berry from *A Timbered Choir: The Sabbath Poems 1979–1997.* Reprinted by permission of Counterpoint.

Book design by Drew Stevens
Cover design by designpointinc.com

First edition
Published by Westminster John Knox Press
Louisville, Kentucky

This book is printed on acid-free paper that meets the American National Standards Institute Z39.48 standard. ∞

PRINTED IN THE UNITED STATES OF AMERICA

08 09 10 11 12 13 14 15 16 17 — 10 9 8 7 6 5 4 3 2 1

Stone, Bryan P.
    Sabbath in the city : sustaining urban pastoral excellence / Bryan P. Stone and Claire E. Wolfteich.
    — 1st ed.
        p. cm.
    Includes bibliographical references and indexes.
    ISBN 978-0-664-23349-5 (alk. paper)
    1. City clergy—Religious life. 2. City churches. 3. Church work. I. Wolfteich, Claire E. II. Title.

    BV637.5.S76 2008
    253'.09173'2—dc22

                                                                    2008008571

Sabbath in the City

Dedicated to the ninety-six pastors who were the source and inspiration for this book and from whom we have learned invaluable lessons about the city, Sabbath, and friendship

Contents

Introduction

This book grew out of a project called "Sustaining Urban Pastoral Excellence" conducted by Boston University School of Theology and its Center for Practical Theology. Generously funded by the Lilly Endowment, Inc., the project invited Christian pastors from around the nation to participate in a program designed to sustain excellent ministry by strengthening practices of spiritual renewal, study and reflection, and partnership. Central also to the program was our offer of a four- to eight-week period of compensated leave from congregational duties. We ended up working with ninety-six pastors from twenty-four partnerships across the nation in six-month cycles. Our partnerships represented an amazing cross section of the United States, including Aurora (IL), Baltimore (MD), Bangor (ME), Birmingham (AL), Boston (MA), Bridgeport (CT), Chattanooga (TN), Chicago (IL), El Paso (TX), Hampton Roads (VA), Hartford (CT), Los Angeles (CA), New York (NY), Portland (OR), Salt Lake City (UT), San Diego (CA), Savannah (GA), Seattle (WA), Springfield (MA), and Syracuse (NY). The project was designed both as a program of support for urban pastors and as a research project, which sought answers to two primary questions: (1) what *constitutes* pastoral excellence in the urban context and (2) what *sustains* it?

The project focused on four key areas that we originally hypothesized as contributing to healthy and vibrant ministry in the city: partnership, Sabbath, study, and spiritual renewal.

1. **Partnership.** Pastors frequently say they experience isolation. At the heart of the program, therefore, were four-member partnerships composed of pastoral leaders from

the same city, who applied to the program together. During the six-month cycle in which they participated, the pastors met biweekly for fellowship, support, accountability, study, renewal, and sharing.

2. **Spiritual Renewal.** Each of the partnerships developed plans for its own spiritual renewal during the six-month cycle, including individual and group practices integrated with its biweekly meetings and sabbatical leave time.

3. **Sabbath**. Urban pastors may experience burnout and exhaustion without implementing healthy, biblical rhythms of work, play, rest, and renewal. The project funded sabbatical leave time for each pastor and was instrumental in helping all of them to focus on flexible, creative, and sustainable "Sabbath" practices such as art, recreation, journaling, prayer, travel, reading, and fellowship that help bring balance and wholeness to life and ministry.

4. **Study**. Each partnership identified one key question to pursue in depth during the cycle of participation—a question of interest to the entire group and representative of the kinds of issues or questions that each pastor faces in his or her own unique urban environment. Some of the study questions focused on immigration, violence and peace making, multicultural ministry, clergy and church "divides," congregational growth and decline in the urban context, race and reconciliation, and urban networking.

Among the many highlights of the program, especially important were the opportunities to bring the pastors to Boston and to the School of Theology campus at the beginning and end of their six-month cycles to interact with faculty, students, and staff. Students preparing to enter the ministry were able to catch a passion for urban ministry directly from the pastors themselves, and the seminary community as a whole benefited from gaining new perspectives on the issues facing urban pastors and their congregations as well as lessons learned in attempting to sustain ministry in the city. As project codirectors, we were also able to visit each of the urban sites to see more closely the context in which the pastors work.

This intentionally urban focus of the project has been important throughout. When we originally began to consider how we could contribute to the Lilly Endowment's national project focused on pastoral excellence, we began to think about the unique particularities of our own context. Our campus snakes its way through the city of Boston, with the Charles River at our backs and the hustle and bustle of Commonwealth Avenue and a busy trolley line right outside our front doors. We wanted to be more intentional as a school about how we respond to the urban environment in the ways we teach, learn, and conduct research. For despite the fact that the vast majority of pastors minister in urban contexts today, ministerial education still operates as if the city has very little impact on the way ministry is carried out or on the way pastors are prepared for ministry. For example, one of the things that was reinforced to us by urban pastors is that "pastoral care" means much more than the traditional roles of counseling, preaching, worship leadership, and caring for parishioners and their families throughout the cycles of life. Rather, these pastors tend to think of pastoral care in ways that include meeting of social needs along a remarkable continuum that includes everything from food, clothing, and education to job training, legal aid, and community organizing. The urban context *should* affect what seminaries teach and how they teach.

In an effort to identify what constitutes and what sustains excellent pastoral ministry in urban contexts, we listened to and learned from our participating pastors and we also visited and talked with many other urban pastors and ministry professionals throughout the nation and, of course, tried to integrate all this with existing research on the subject. As pastors shared with us their understanding of excellence, we were affirmed in believing that many of the marks of excellence are not unique to urban ministry but instead apply to all ministry. Even so, the complexity, diversity, and intensity of urban life press in on pastors in ways that present enormous challenges and opportunities, which in turn shape the unique patterns of "excellence" that characterize their lives and ministries.

WHAT WE LEARNED

First, we learned that excellent urban pastors *love* their cities. They have a heart for the city. They see the city not primarily as something to be fixed or as a problem to be solved, but as a gift and as a living organism that by its very nature magnifies both creativity and deviance. For this reason, excellent urban pastors learn how to minister *with* their cities, rather than merely *in* their cities or *to* their cities.[1] With Jeremiah 29:7, they understand that their own *shalom* is bound up with the *shalom* of the cities where God has sent them; and in this way, their lives and ministries are greatly contextualized by urban life.

Not every person who enters pastoral ministry is "wired" for city life. Cities are characterized by overcrowding, violence, pollution, noise, diversity, anonymity, a rapid pace of life, high concentrations of poverty and need, powerlessness in the face of impersonal systems, and lots of steel and concrete. No wonder some pastors in urban areas see themselves as "doing time" until they can land that beautiful church out in the "burbs." There is, moreover, no universal experience of the city among urban pastors. Some see it as a dry place, full of need and parched for God's Spirit. But most of the pastors we have worked with delight in being there and their hearts seem to beat to the pulse of the city. They come alive when we ask them to talk about it. It is a wonderful experience to tour a city with pastors who have a passion and love for it . . . and especially to tour a city with pastors who know where to eat! One of the rewarding side benefits of directing a project like ours and of being able to conduct site visits is that we now know some of the best eating spots across the nation, from the taquerias of El Paso to the crab shacks of Baltimore to the barbecue establishments of Chattanooga and Birmingham.

Second, we have learned that excellent urban pastors *know* their cities. They know how their cities operate. They know its demographics and its changing demographic patterns. They know who the community leaders are—the gatekeepers, informants, resource persons, and individuals with connections. They understand the way money and power flow into (though too often out of) the city. They know the programs and social services that are available, and they know what the most pressing issues within their communities are. Excellent urban pastors tend to have a deep understanding of their contexts and a wise sense of how to carry the gospel to people in their particular life situations. They also have a hunger to know more.

This knowledge derives from reading, studying, interviews, and other more formal means such as attending seminars and workshops on urban issues. But it is also characterized by a practical knowledge, a *wisdom* that is derived from shared insight, participation in neighborhood watches, school boards, and showing up at council meetings. It comes from participating in cultural activities that, as Craig French, from Syracuse, New York, put so aptly, "move us beyond ourselves, providing beauty, pleasure, inspiration, information, and new perspectives . . . [that] force us to slow down, stop, look around and ponder."

To know and to love the city, of course, means also to know and love *the people* of the city and to practice a solidarity with them that creates a space for confession, pardon, and forgiveness. To know and love the people of the city is to treat no one like a heathen, a demon, or an outcast, and this honoring of "the other" we encounter allows us first to hear them; second, to serve them; and third, to be open to allowing them to creatively transform our ministries. Coming to know parishioners as well as other persons in the community is increasingly difficult given the fact that people are more mobile and more difficult to connect with. While this book is not a how-to manual for urban ministry or an attempt to distill the vast storehouse of knowledge about urban life and ministry from our participating pastors (on average, the pastors we studied had spent between fifteen and twenty years each in urban ministry), chapter 1 will identify some of the more prominent challenges and opportunities that characterize the urban context of pastoral ministry.

Third, we learned that urban pastoral excellence is sustained through collegial partnerships that emphasize mutual sharing and support, a common project or task, camaraderie, and communal spiritual formation. Because of the complexity of urban life, excellent urban pastors know that their ministry with the city must occur on multiple levels. In order to be effective, urban pastors know how various urban systems work and how to work the systems. For that and other reasons, networking is an essential practice for excellent urban pastors. The pastor who networks effectively is often better able to discern where God's Spirit is already at work and has already planted a vision. She or he can see signposts of God's reign wherever they might be. Such networking is not only about exchanging information and ideas—though that is vital—but also about developing relationships of sharing, support, and solidarity. Building such relationships is not always easy nor does it come naturally. Many urban pastors find themselves trying to minister in the midst of long-standing disagreements and divides, even and especially among clergy who have been unable to form united vision or partnership when working, for example, with municipal governments, school boards, and agencies.

But excellent urban pastors know where in their cities to find potential ministry partners—not only in other churches, but also in governmental and social agencies as well as cultural, business, and artistic communities. Because of scarce means, they understand they must pool resources and create a climate of mutual support in which the whole is greater than the sum of its parts. Urban pastors seek out commonalities and concrete pathways toward sharing as a way of overcoming a debilitating sense of competition. As Mark Smith of Aurora, Illinois, put it, by combining resources, gifts, focuses, and the like, the church becomes a living organism that can more effectively meet the varying needs of the community.

This emphasis on partnership and networking that we saw in studying urban pastors was nowhere more evident than in the friendships that developed among the pastors themselves in the four-person partnerships around which our program was structured. Alongside practices of Sabbath keeping, *friendship* may be one of the most important and essential practices that surfaced in all that we watched and heard pastors saying and doing throughout the life of our project. Most of us rarely think about *cultivating* friendships until we need friends. We may not often think of friendship as a discipline, a practice, or a skill to be learned and developed—perhaps because friendship is among the most normal and important of life practices that ordinary people do. Yet it is a practice that many pastors quit practicing soon after entering ministry. In chapter 2, we discuss pastoral friendship in the urban context and the importance of finding partners in whom pastors can trust and with whom they can bare their souls in the context of safety, mutual accountability, and support.

A fourth lesson we have learned is that pastoral excellence is constituted by habits, practices, rhythms, and relationships that shape both the character of the pastor and his or her performance of ministerial duties. Many of these we have come to speak of in terms of the more comprehensive discipline of "Sabbath keeping." While an extended period of sabbatical leave was central to our project, it was but one aspect of a larger set of practices of Sabbath keeping that pastors described as transformative, as opening up new perspectives, as connected to a newfound sense of freedom, as offering needed rest, as restorative of interests and passions long neglected, and as fostering healthier self-care and family relationships. In chapters 3 and 4, we explore Sabbath keeping and other practices of spiritual renewal that have proved to be important to nourishing the ministry of urban pastors, and in chapter 5 we suggest ways that Christians might cultivate an "urban spirituality."

Fifth, we have learned that pastors, early on as ministerial students, need to develop these habits, practices, rhythms, and relationships, or else they may never develop them at all. This coincides with our belief that the seminary experience often fails to model and reinforce them and, in fact, models a way of life that is likely to lead to burnout, dysfunction, and a diminished sense of joy and vocation in pastoral ministry. While this book does not provide an in-depth treatment of how seminaries might better provide a context in which pastors early on can develop the necessary resources for sustaining pastoral excellence, we offer some practical suggestions in the conclusion of the book.

ON EXCELLENCE

It may be useful at the outset to say a few words about the term "excellence." Frankly speaking, many of the pastors participating in our project expressed ambivalence about the word and its connotations in relation to Christian ministry. For one thing, no pastor ever fulfills his or her vocation perfectly just as no congregation ever fulfills its mission perfectly. Talk of "excellence," therefore, might seem to run counter to the humility that is at the heart of the gospel. One pastor suggested that if we can use the term excellence to describe Christian pastors, it is an excellence that is more about brokenness and cruciform discipleship than about "doing more." There is a death to self that pastors reported to us in various ways as being at the core of pastoral excellence. But it is not a death *of* self that comes through busy-ness, depletion, exhaustion, and overextending oneself. On the contrary, it is a death *to* self in the sense of letting go, being able to say no, and releasing the stranglehold pastors sometimes think they need to keep on their congregations and ministries.

In employing the word "excellence," it is important to remember that the Greek word translated as excellence in the New Testament (*areté*) could just as well be translated "virtue"—and in this way, it should be noted, humility does not stand in contrast to excellence. On the contrary, as a primary Christian virtue humility is an example of excellence. We could, then, just as well speak of our project as "sustaining urban pastoral *virtue*." To do that may actually be helpful since the word "excellence" has been so taken over by utilitarian or consumerist modes of thinking, such that something is excellent when it fulfills some external purpose, satisfies some desire, or meets some need.

But the kind of excellence we have found in urban pastors is something quite different. It is not defined by how many programs are run, how many converts are made, or how witty one's sermons are. For most of our pastors, a commitment to excellence is not the same as attempting to go first-class in all that they or their congregations do. Pastoral excellence is instead a virtue shaped and nurtured by practices that continually bring a pastor into connection with the source of all holiness. Virtuous pastors recognize and affirm as sacred their own longing for spiritual nurture, for community, for knowledge, and for time simply to "be." They incorporate practices of prayer, renewal, friendship, presence, Sabbath, and study into the particular demands of their context. These practices are not distractions from ministry, luxuries to be tolerated, but rather key dimensions of what it means continually to grow into the life of disciple and pastor.

All of this is but another way of emphasizing the importance of seeking and sustaining an "urban spirituality" that is attuned to discovering and creating necessary rhythms, patterns, and practices that nourish the pastor's spirit and the spirits of his parishioners. The notion of an urban spirituality, which we take up in chapter 5, is more art than science and is a distinctive style of living and of integrating the experience and knowledge of God with the complexities of the urban world.

Not all of the qualities of excellent urban pastors are unique to city life. Many are transferable and are probably true of pastoral excellence in just about any situation. But city life has an extraordinary intensity, pace, and complexity. Whether or not urban ministry requires a distinctive set of competencies, virtues, relationships, and imagination, it is a distinctive vocation, both intensely demanding and equally rewarding. It is our prayer that God will never stop calling urban pastors, gifting them, and giving them vision, and that the church will ever increase its support and encouragement of their work.

WITH APPRECIATION

The Sustaining Urban Pastoral Excellence project could not have been undertaken without the support, generosity, and hard work of numerous persons. We are, of course, grateful to the Lilly Endowment, Inc.—to Craig Dykstra, John Wimmer, and to the staff of the Sustaining Pastoral Excellence Coordination Office at Duke Divinity School, all of whom have encouraged us and helped us realize our vision. We are of course indebted to the ninety-six pastors who participated in the Sustaining Urban Pastoral Excellence program over the past five years and for their permission to quote from their written applications and reports as well as from the transcripts of our oral interviews with them. We are especially thankful to Kristin White, who served as our project coordinator, providing daily oversight and facilitation to literally every aspect of the project, including travel, reimbursement, conferences, record keeping, and communication. It would be impossible to summarize the many accolades and expressions of appreciation for Kristin that have come to us from participating pastors. There could not have been a harder working, more personable, or more caring coordinator, nor could there have been a more effective liaison between Boston University School of Theology and our urban pastors. We are also indebted to Nikita McCalister and to Xochitl Alvizo, who served as student interns on the project. Nikita and Xochitl are already creative and visionary ministers and theologians in their own right, and they worked incredibly hard to recruit pastors, process their applications, assist in coordination of travel and events, and follow up with interviews and research. Finally, we wish to thank the many student assistants and researchers, both paid and volunteer, who helped us throughout the project, notably Shemia Fagan, Julian Gotobed,

Niki Johnson, and Doug Knutson. Special thanks to Kathryn House, who did an extensive job of culling through notes, reports, transcripts, applications, and interviews, transforming a sea of data into something more manageable and thematically organized.

1

Urban Challenge and Opportunity

But seek the welfare of the city where I have sent you into exile, and pray to the Lord on its behalf, for in its welfare you will find your welfare.

(Jer. 29:7)

May 23, 2007, was an important day in the history of the human species. It was the day the world turned urban. Based on United Nations calculations that the world would be 51.3 percent urban by 2010 and using average daily urban population increases from 2005 to 2010, social scientists and demographers projected May 23 as the transition date when the world urban population finally went over the 50 percent mark.[1] While this transition might appear to have been a long, slow process, considering the whole of human history, urbanization is, of course, a rather recent and rapid phenomenon. In fact, it was only in the past 107 years that the world's urban population leapt from 13 percent to 50 percent.[2] Ancient Rome may well have boasted over a million residents in the first century (a population that was eventually decimated by disease and invasion), but London in 1820 would be the first city in the world after that to have a million residents. By 2020 the world will have five hundred cities with more than a million people. In fact, dozens of megacities already host millions of residents. With a population of thirty-five million, for example, greater Tokyo by itself has a population larger than that of the entire nation of Canada.

1

The United States has been urbanized for some time now, having "gone urban" in the late 1910s. Currently 79 percent of the U.S. population lives in an urban context.[3] That statistic may not be surprising for anyone who has driven across miles and miles of empty prairie, forest, desert, or farmland and who has been impressed with the vastness of uninhabited land. Of the total U.S. land base, only 3 percent is used for residential, commercial, utility, and other urban uses. The rest is classified as rural and is anything from farms, pastures, and ranges to deserts, parks, forests, or wetlands.[4]

As human beings increasingly huddle together in dense, urban space, tremendous opportunities and challenges present themselves. That is because the phenomenon of urbanization is much more than a matter of population increases or density. It has to do with distinctive forms of human relationship, interconnection, and complex patterns of cultural, economic, and political life that transcend the close-knit patterns of smaller communities. The church, however, is not always aware of the opportunities nor is it well equipped to respond to the challenges of urbanization. Models of the church and of pastoral ministry characteristically reflect a rural and agrarian past. Indeed, the very word "pastor" comes from the Latin for "shepherd," reflecting the rural context for ministry out of which it first arose. Likewise, the primary exemplars of church vitality and congregational development held up before pastors today are typically those developed in suburban contexts at the edges of the city, while inner city churches are left to decline and eventually to die.

If the church lags in its awareness of and response to the challenges and opportunities of urban life, seminaries and divinity schools are equally delinquent in preparing pastoral leadership for urban congregations. According to a 1997 study conducted by Robert Kemper, only one-third of all seminaries in the United States accredited by the Association of Theological Schools offer courses related to urban ministry.[5] Whether reluctant to accept the fact of urbanization or oblivious to the relevance of urban life for how Christians do theology, worship, seek God, or embody their witness in the world, both churches and seminaries remain stubbornly out of touch with what is now one of the most all-encompassing and important features of contemporary human existence.

The pervasiveness of urban life is reason enough for being more intentional about sustaining excellent ministry in the urban context, but it is also true that Christianity was itself originally a largely urban movement and that the New Testament reflects this urban bias. The titles of many of the documents that make up the New Testament reveal just how urban Christianity was, addressed as they were to urbanites. But, alas, our overfamiliarity with those titles has caused us to forget this fact. If the apostle Paul had lived in the twenty-first century in the United States, Christians might memorize passages from *San Diegans* instead of *Ephesians* and meditate on *Bostonians* instead of *Colossians.* Perhaps we would study the *Angelinos* correspondence instead of the *Corinthian,* and preachers might take as their text something from *First* or *Second New Yorkers.*

All things considered, the New Testament is a remarkably urban book. It has much to say about how the church lives together in the context of economic disparities, social and cultural divisions, and the radical diversity one is likely to find today in urban contexts. Even the Revelation to John is addressed to urban churches—or more precisely it is addressed to the urban "angels" associated with those churches ("to the angel of Philadelphia," "to the angel of Smyrna," etc.). Indeed, the hope of the people of God is often imagined throughout Scripture in urban terms as the "city of God," the "holy habitation" where God dwells (Ps. 46:4) or as the "new Jerusalem," which God has prepared for us and toward which the people of God are on pilgrimage in this world (Heb. 11:16; Rev. 3:12, 21:2). The city, in other words, figures centrally as a symbol of human relations which, when rightly ordered toward God, neighbor, and creation, bears faithful witness to God's glory throughout the nations.

If, however, the city is imagined in Scripture both as the holy habitation of God and as the new creation toward which the people of God are on pilgrimage, it can also be understood as a place of idolatry and injustice. Jesus weeps over Jerusalem; Sodom and Gomorrah become shorthand for wickedness and inhospitality; and the ancient city of Babylon symbolizes evil in the world and hostility against God. Both Jerusalem and Babylon, in fact, become two of the primary biblical symbols for imagining the possibilities of human fulfillment, on the one hand, and its ruination, on the other.

To speak of our own context or of the New Testament as "urban," however, is made difficult by an increasing complexity in defining "urban" today in any strict or univocal sense. Thanks to urban sprawl and the commuter culture spawned by the advent of high-speed, limited-access highways in the 1950s, the continuum between urban, suburban, exurban, and rural has become increasingly difficult to parse. No wonder that the U.S. Census Bureau, rather than simply using the term "urban," now speaks of "urbanized areas"—contiguous, densely settled census blocks of at least one thousand persons per square mile (and other connected blocks) that together encompass a population of at least fifty thousand persons.

But for growing numbers of people, official definitions like this don't capture the most important features of the urban social context. The word "urban" refers to more than statistical population or density. It also refers to a way of life and a network of social relations or an alternate value system, and it is increasingly difficult to define narrowly with reference to the geographical center, or core of a city.[6] For some in the United States, the word "urban" is used symbolically, or as code for nonwhite peoples, and has overtones that reflect racial divisions and stereotyping. The phrase "urban contemporary," for example, was coined by the entertainment industry to refer to a genre of music that includes rap, hip-hop, contemporary R&B, and other styles associated with African American music.

Perhaps many of us define "urban" the way Justice Potter Stewart once defined pornography—"I know it when I see it." "Urban," in other words, is not only a word describing *place*. It is also a word describing the way we "practice place,"[7] and this always has to do with much more than visible geography alone. It includes the way we encounter, walk, order, situate, orient, or temporalize place . . . the way we make places function. The way we "practice place" is the performance of a comprehensive social imagination about the way things *can* be and the way things *should* be in everyday life that carries with it distinct ways of relating to one another, sharing resources, ordering power relations, working, playing, behaving properly, or using time. Excellence in urban pastoral ministry, or so we have found, is characterized by a unique ability to interface an urban practice of place with a Christian practice of place. It is, in other words, the ability to bring a Christian social imagination to life and ministry in the city while simultaneously allowing the distinctive challenges and opportunities of the urban context to creatively shape and contextualize that imagination.

Each urban context is, of course, unique. Ministry in and around Syracuse University will look different from ministry within the Cabrini-Green public housing development on Chicago's near north side. It will look still different from ministry with the homeless on the streets of downtown Boston, or in the tourist-saturated streets of Savannah, Georgia. But among the pastors we have studied who take seriously the task of contextualizing their ministries in today's cities, a cluster of challenges shows up repeatedly as distinctively "urban," regardless of how unique the individual situations may be. Six of the more important of these relate to (1) the experience of multiple transitions, (2) comprehensive social need, (3) negotiating identity, (4) alienation and division, (5) diversity and immigration, and (6) scarcity of resources.

TRANSITION

One of the first widespread challenges faced by urban pastors is how not only to survive, but to grow and flourish as a church in the rapidly changing environment of the city. Given shifting population trends within cities in relation to phenomena such as suburban flight, immigration, plant closings, gentrification, or economic downturns, urban churches constantly find themselves looking for ways to adapt to the changing situations around them. This is especially the case for historic and once prestigious mainline (and largely white) congregations where, as in the case of Bridgeport, Connecticut, loss of the city's industrial base in manufacturing and shipping in the 1960s, the growth of suburbs, the proliferation of suburban shopping malls, and the eventual bankruptcy of the city in the 1980s took a huge toll on the center city. Bridgeport took the same path taken by other older cities in the northeast United States, where the downtown becomes an isolated and lifeless district and a no-go zone after sunset.

Downtown white churches are not the only ones that experience urban transitions, however. For decades historic black churches have witnessed the influx of new populations into their neighborhoods, bringing with them new nationalities, new cultures, new languages, and new racial tensions. So, for example, while in Los Angeles the population of Watts in 1970 was 90 percent black and 8 percent Latino, in 2000 that population was 38 percent black and 61 percent Latino. While the black church has traditionally been a respite and resource for blacks unwelcome in churches defined by racist white norms and values, many of the black pastors we have talked to highlight the challenge of demonstrating welcome to newer immigrant and ethnic groups among whom they now interact daily.

While immigration is a major factor in transitions such as these, demographic shifts typically have many causes. For example, America's population is aging while household sizes are shrinking. Recent attempts at urban development across the nation have also contributed to demographic transitions faced by congregations. As municipalities increasingly focus on transforming run-down corridors or abandoned warehouse districts into vibrant residential, shopping, and entertainment areas, some cities are becoming newly attractive to young professionals, empty nester baby boomers, or others who simply crave an urban lifestyle. Revitalization over the last twenty-five years along the riverfront of Chattanooga, Tennessee, for example, has produced new residential lofts, an arts district, population growth, and increased tourism. While Chattanooga has received numerous citations as an example of "best practices" in urban development, the poor in such instances do not simply disappear and are often merely displaced. Impoverished neighborhoods near revitalized city centers can become even more impoverished.

One type of congregational response to these urban transitions is simply to grow older and smaller. Here the image of the church is that of a fortress, embattled against or untouched by the surrounding community. Other congregations in a similar position will rent out space to congregations that better reflect the demographic transitions in the surrounding community. Another response is to relocate—the military model, where the church pulls up stakes and moves to another base of operation (though in fact, it is only the facility that is relocating; the people packed up and moved long ago). Yet another response is something more like a parish model where the church sees itself as belonging to its community and as living in symbiosis with it. Here the church embraces community change as part of its own identity and seeks to be intentional about recontextualizing its worship, its ministries, and indeed its very presence in the community. But even if a congregation chooses the latter, urban pastors often face the challenge of guiding congregations through transition with a lack of stable leadership and economic resources, dilapidated buildings that are an economic drain, and other infrastructure limitations such as shortage of parking or the facility's designation as a historical landmark, so that potential alterations are greatly restricted. Then, too, most churches do not take transition seriously until it is too late.

The urban pastors that served as our co-researchers have wrestled especially with how to become communities of faith capable of inviting new generations of Christians. Urban churches in the midst of transition often find themselves facing one of the following common scenarios: (1) a majority of the membership (as many as 90 percent in some cases) driving

in from the suburbs, without a natural sense of being stake-
holders in the local community, or (2) an aging membership
that remained in the city despite the flight of others to the suburbs. In the second case, as these older members become fewer
and fewer, the newer and younger members the church is able
to attract (as difficult as that is in the first place) have little time
to devote to church work, and so it often becomes difficult to
form a strong leadership core from among the very people who
could revitalize and bring new vision and energy to the church.
Despite the ever-changing patterns of urban demographics,
pastors of urban churches report feeling pressure from denominational superiors, congregation members, and their own
peers to make sure their churches stay the same or grow, without loss of membership.

Theological, ministerial, leadership, and worship resources
to help urban pastors and their churches through transitions
such as these are not always easy to find. As noted by several of
the pastors we interviewed, prevailing models of church growth
and leadership development extolled in Christian circles are
typically those oriented toward suburban communities—Wil-
low Creek Community or Saddleback Valley mega-church
models. As Jennifer Gutierrez, of Los Angeles, noted, many of
these models "are not well suited for a much more ethnically
and economically diverse demographic that faces completely
different life questions."

One thing is certain: urban churches that are intentional
about remaining and thriving in the city must be committed
and open to change. Indeed, some of the congregations that not
only survive but thrive in the city have come to see their relationship to the ever-changing urban context as a pilgrimage[8]—
as an opportunity to be embraced hopefully rather than an
obstacle to be hurdled. Pastors who embrace change rather than
resisting it also speak of the virtues of being proactive, creative,
and mission-focused in relation to change rather than merely
reactive. An excellent urban pastor is one who can tolerate
ambiguity and has a relative comfort with a high degree of
chaos. As Joan Murray, of Boston, told us, "In the urban con-

text, ministry calls for change. We must adapt, transition, rearrange, or reshape. Whatever it takes, we must develop a climate conducive to accepting change in order to offer a relevant response to the community's needs." This means a willingness to learn new things, to visit other churches, and to explore new ideas, strategies, paradigms, and approaches to key areas of ministry. This question of being proactive rather than reactive overlaps with the question of identity discussed later in this chapter. The pastoral challenge is to be an agent of change guided by authenticity and a clear sense of giftedness and vocation rather than being pulled in a dozen different directions by the ever-changing winds of transition and congregational expectations fueled by the slogan, "The pastor is key."

There may be no place to "stand" in the city . . . or certainly no place to stand still. But one of the empowering messages heard repeatedly from urban pastors is that in the midst of transition it is important to remember that the church is God's, not ours. This confidence is not a cause for detachment or carelessness, but the basis for going forward boldly with study, planning, regular and continuing reevaluation, and prayerful seeking of God's vision in each new situation.

COMPREHENSIVE SOCIAL NEED

Given that there are more than three hundred thousand religious congregations in the United States, making them the most widespread institution in the nation, it may not be surprising that, according to a recent study, "Clergy and congregations are the number one place Americans turn to when they have serious problems, more than the government or human and health service professionals."[9] In fact, three-quarters of all congregations in the United States have some mechanism for helping people in economic need. Nowhere is this truer than in urban congregations where pastors and their congregations often find themselves attending to a wide range of social issues that are virtually impossible to summarize easily, including poverty and widespread economic disparity; crime; unemployment; drugs; industry closings; homelessness; gang violence; lack of affordable health care; racism and segregation; immigration; the treatment of seniors, of those who are mentally ill, and of ex-offenders; teen pregnancy and lack of family and social support for teenage parents; inadequate support systems for preteens, which often leads to violent crime; overworked or absent parents; and substandard public schools.

Letty Russell has suggested that it may be useful to consider the city as "battered woman." "Like a battered woman," says Russell, "the city suffers through cycles of violence, isolation, and fear. Like a battered woman, in suffering those cycles, the city often cries out to us in silent and not-so-silent screams."[10] Also like a battered woman, not only is the city caught in a cycle of violence, but the city is held responsible for it: "Blamed as sinful, immoral, decadent, and dirty, the city is seen as anything but the victim of violence, abused by the very forces of economics and politics that have been the source of her strength and culture."[11] Pastoral responses to the social needs of the city, therefore—as with responses to battered women—may well begin with immediate and emergency interventions, but must inevitably take into account the complex and interlocking structures of violence and injustice that both create and perpetuate those needs.

In the ninety-six urban congregations we visited over a five-year period, what we saw firsthand was a mind-boggling array of social services and congregational ministries delivered both professionally by pastors and other paid staff and through voluntary efforts by church members in response to these needs. At its most basic level, pastoral responses to comprehensive social need take the form of what are sometimes called works of mercy or acts of charity—emergency assistance in the shape of food pantries or hot meals, clothing closets, help with utility payments and rent, adult day care, medical care and shelter for the homeless, and ministries to persons with HIV/AIDS and their families.[12] It is easy to become cynical and numb when faced with the same needs day after day; pastors who effectively engage in these ministries, therefore, often have a well-developed sense of patience, freely opening their hands day after day to "the poor and needy neighbor," since "there will never cease to be some in need on the earth" (Deut. 15:11). Among the many marks of excellence that characterize urban pastors is a charity that is creative, deeply committed, willing to stay with the conversation, and born of patient listening, vulnerability, and a dependable presence.

Of course, *charity* as a response to human need can be superficial, cheap, and painless—a condescending substitute for solidarity with those who suffer. If cities are complex entities with interlocking systems, the nature of poverty and oppression in cities is equally complex and systemic. Frustrated with trying to get a handle on these systems so as to address them, well-meaning Christians avoid matters of structural injustice, finding it far easier to focus only on symptoms. The poor become the "unfortunate" or the "less privileged" rather than the oppressed or sinned-against. Compassion is reduced to pity and, instead of justice, the poor get Christmas baskets. This kind of charity is too often little more than an attempt to relieve our feelings of guilt, establish credit for ourselves in the wider community, or make us feel good because of our kindness and decency toward our fellow human beings. Paulo Freire offers a helpful distinction at this point between true generosity and false charity:

> True generosity consists precisely in fighting to destroy the causes which nourish false charity. False charity constrains the fearful and subdued, the "rejects of life," to extend their trembling hands. True generosity lies in striving so that these hands—whether of individuals or entire peoples—need be extended less and less in supplication, so that more and more they become human hands which work and, working, transform the world.[13]

Genuine charity, then, remains an essential first step in responding pastorally to social need, both for the sake of those who suffer and, indeed, for the sake of our own need to open ourselves in love to others. But in keeping with Freire's distinction, what we find in urban churches just as frequently as acts of charity are ministries of empowerment that attempt to ensure that human hands "need be extended less and less in supplication." While ministries of charity attempt to provide the necessities of human life (food, clothing, shelter, etc.), ministries of empowerment seek to enable others to lead their lives with dignity, voice, and agency, thereby breaking out of cycles of dependency and helplessness. Without the dimension of empowerment in urban pastoral ministry, charity would become little more than a Band-Aid and could even perpetuate poverty and dependency.

Here are just a few of the ministries of empowerment we saw in urban churches: recreational and educational programs; congregational health and parish nursing ministries; low-income home ownership or home repair programs; community gardens; day camps for children and youth; music and arts programs; comprehensive ministries for unwed teenage mothers; youth mentoring, after-school, and student scholarship programs; counseling services of all kinds; creative art and film ministries for the homeless that minister to their social, spiritual, and intellectual needs; credit unions; alcohol and drug recovery programs; adult education classes including language programs and high-school equivalency certification; marriage workshops; and job training.

Beyond charity and empowerment, however, there is a third level of Christian ministry that figures prominently in urban churches. If urban pastors are challenged not only to "give a person a fish, so she will eat for a day," but to "teach a person to fish, so she will eat for a lifetime," the pastors we interviewed were also deeply concerned about the fishing conditions—about free and full access to the fishing hole and about freedom from pollution upstream. Urban pastors regularly speak of their engagement in ministries of social justice and of being faced with the challenge of exposing injustice and confronting the principalities and powers in this regard. As Hannah Arendt once put it, "Poverty itself is a political, not a natural phenomenon, the result of violence and violation rather than of scarcity."[14]

Alongside ministries of charity and empowerment, some of the justice ministries offered by urban churches are pro bono legal counseling, tenants' and other neighborhood associations, youth advocacy in juvenile court, eco-justice ministries such as recycling or other greening efforts, restorative justice in the form of victim-offender reconciliation and mediation programs, faith-based community organizing, and mobilizing for fair trade. Of course, pastoral ministry in the form of justice work is in many respects difficult to envision and implement because justice and injustice both pertain to complex social systems and structures, economic policies, and other patterns of trade and commerce. Identifying the source of the problem is as difficult as finding ways toward healing and repair. Urban pastors identify the posture of solidarity with those who have been victimized or marginalized by oppressive structures as a necessary starting point for this kind of work, both for gaining perspective and for earning the trust of those on whose behalf urban churches protest, advocate, and organize.

When you visit urban churches engaged in meeting social needs at so many levels, what quickly becomes clear is why they are seven-day-a-week churches. What is equally clear is why urban pastoral ministry is characterized not only by direct and personal forms of ministerial intervention but also by the cultivation of relationships, solidarity, and networks within the city and a multi-layered approach to social need that includes not only personal but communal well-being.

A caution is in order at this point, however. In addition to being busied with organizing ministries, mobilizing resources, lobbying city hall, and so on, clergy also have to negotiate attitudes of parishioners who may see them as having lost their pastoral touch. One of the greatest challenges in urban pastoral ministry, therefore, is discerning one's own priorities for ministry, since it is easy to get burned out trying to be everything to everybody in the midst of overwhelming need. Some pastors, such as Albert Rice of Boston, reported having to exercise particular diligence in limiting the number of social, political, and other ministry-related activities they engage in. As Rice says, limiting his civic involvement "has proven to be very helpful because in doing these things I am a better pastor and family man, and I am preserving myself to be around longer." Urban pastors, in other words, must remain constant in discerning the difference between what they *can* do and what others are *asking* them to do, on the one hand, and what God is *calling* them to do, on the other.

IDENTITY

A second challenge faced by urban pastors is that of negotiating or renegotiating congregational identity, which, of course, also translates into questions of pastoral identity. The urban context is a place where people are able to form multiple relationships and connect with one another in myriad ways that transcend the particular ties that unite them in otherwise provincial communities. At the same time, this diversity and interrelatedness as well as the aforementioned transitions create a situation in which identities are always being created and re-created, negotiated and renegotiated, contested and defended.

One of the challenges of identity faced by urban pastors surfaces in relation to declining denominational loyalties. Many urban pastors mention the struggle of trying to be a congregation that is vital, new, and contextually relevant while at the same time attempting to maintain denominational and local church heritages—and in this endeavor they are very much in the same boat as their nonurban counterparts. The pressure to be relevant is often more than merely a matter of contextualization. The logic of consumerism is pervasive in American culture, and when worship, evangelism, and ministry have been taken over by a prevailing market logic, the pastor becomes not so much the leader of a community of faith or a prophet summoning that community to greater faithfulness in discipleship, as a sales person trying to market a product. The congregation in turn sees itself not primarily as the people of God but as a group of demanding consumers whose desires often conflict with one another and whose lives are connected by little more than the set of choices they have in common. The gospel is transformed into a message people are willing to buy.

In the case of urban congregations, however, there is the additional feature of the ever-changing racial and socioeconomic makeup of their neighborhoods, which often results in a growing incompatibility between a church's sense of who it is and the realities of its surrounding community. Music and cultural aesthetics are perennial points of conflict for urban churches in this regard. For many parishioners in historically English-speaking congregations, the incorporation of other language groups in worship has not felt like a successful outreach strategy but, as one pastor put it, more like a "hostile takeover," even though the transitions in the church simply mirror the transitions already taking place in the surrounding neighborhood. So closely can ethnic and cultural identities become associated with ecclesiological or liturgical commitments that, as observed by Altagracia Pérez, an Episcopal priest from Los Angeles, parishioners can begin to question their congregation's transition in terms of whether they are giving up on being "truly Episcopalian" or being forced to give up the best of their "Anglican heritage." Again, the challenge here is one of identity.

Some urban pastors mention the challenge of trying to mix parishioners who commute in from the suburbs to which they moved and those from the surrounding urban context who may live in closer proximity to the church but who play fewer significant leadership roles in the church. The "absentee landlordism" of key members of an urban congregation is a reality mentioned by many pastors as contributing to questions of identity, and at times this can turn into alienation or even outright hostility between a congregation and its immediate context, with members staying away from night meetings or criticisms from the neighborhood about the church's lack of concern and engagement. When a congregation has purposed to remain in ministry with its community rather than relocating, what is the place of those members who drive in for church but who don't live in the community the rest of the time?

Yet a further challenge with regard to identity, as we have already seen, stems from the reality that an urban church is often expected to be, and perhaps needs to be, more than a traditional church—something more like a comprehensive community center where a whole range of needs are met. Urban pastors we interviewed consistently describe their work as about equally divided between those who are formal members or regular attendees of the church and those who are not. Sometimes a church is called on to serve many purposes and to connect persons in need with a variety of social and human services, if not providing those services itself. For immigrant populations, the church frequently serves as a "landing pad"— a first-stop, one-stop, full-service agent of socialization and enculturation. As J. L. Carter, a pastor from Baltimore, said, "I am not just a pastor of the congregation, but I am a pastor of the community."

The ecclesiological questions at stake here are complex. On the one hand, the church risks losing its identity as a called-out people, a gathered, worshiping, and embodied witness to God's reign by reducing itself to a mere provider of social services. On the other hand, the church as the body of Christ is called to love the world as Christ loved the world, and it is difficult to see how that can be done without concrete ministries of compassion, empowerment, and justice. No wonder urban congregations, like their pastors, often find themselves asking, Who are we? What are we?

DIVERSITY AND IMMIGRATION

One of the chief differences between rural or suburban contexts, on the one hand, and urban contexts, on the other, is the relatively homogeneous social makeup of the former in contrast to the socioeconomic, ethnic, and cultural diversity of the latter. Indeed, "if there is any one characteristic that typifies the city, it is its plural nature."[15] Though Christian churches as a whole still lag far behind their neighborhoods and other community institutions (such as public schools) in reflecting urban heterogeneity,[16] diversity is consistently cited by urban pastors as one of the most important challenges to their ministries and to their congregations. As Brian Schofield-Bodt, pastor of Golden Hill United Methodist Church in Bridgeport, Connecticut, describes his church, "We have enough diversity here to irritate everybody." As Schofield-Bodt also told us, however, diversity is not only a challenge and an irritation but also a gift and an opportunity—and this was affirmed by virtually all of the pastors we studied. For those urban congregations willing to celebrate diversity and to embrace it, the possibilities for enriched worship, effective outreach, new theological horizons, and the development of a dynamic, multitextured community are virtually endless.

While the sources of diversity experienced by urban congregations are multiple (age, gender, sexuality, race, culture, ability, etc.), immigration shows up repeatedly in pastoral reflections on ministry and places high on any list of important issues that urban pastors say they face in their ministries. Of the close to 290 million residents of the United States, about 12 percent were reported in 2003 as being foreign-born.[17] Immigration has always shaped cities like Miami (58 percent foreign-born), Los Angeles (40 percent), San Francisco (35 percent), or New York (35 percent), which have traditionally been gateways into the United States.[18] But congregations in much smaller cities increasingly see significant numbers of both documented and undocumented foreign-born residents, especially in southern states, where questions of how to respond to the spiritual, material, and social needs of immigrants now become urgent.

Not all urban contexts are the same, of course, when it comes to the impact of immigration. Six of the pastors in our project from New York City were members of the Moravian Church in North America, all of them drawing their membership from Caribbean immigrant populations who first began to arrive in New York at the turn of the twentieth century. This pan-Caribbean demographic significantly shapes the types of ministries in which the church is engaged and how it worships, despite great similarity in Moravian liturgy from church to church. The diverse national origins of members and visitors can add layers of cultural expectation to something as seemingly simple as a communion ritual—expectations that are impossible fully to satisfy. At First Moravian Church in Manhattan, for example, pastor Frank Barker counts no less than thirteen nationalities present in his worship services with Spanish, Dutch, Xhosa, Miskitu, and English all spoken as native languages.

Almost any church in the urban context will be challenged by how best to respond to the needs of immigrant populations, but perhaps nowhere in the United States are the day-to-day realities of immigration-based diversity more apparent than they are in El Paso, Texas, the largest U.S. city along "La Frontera" (the borderland) that stretches three hundred miles wide and two thousand miles long from Brownsville, Texas, to San Diego, California. With a population of seven hundred thousand, El Paso's 27 percent foreign-born population is already significant, but this statistic fails to capture the fact that El Paso is part of the largest shared urban space (with Juárez, Mexico) between the United States and another country, with a combined metropolitan population spanning the two borders of well over two million. El Paso's rapid growth without accompanying prosperity, its demographic shifts (over two-thirds of its residents are now Hispanic), and its volatility around the politics of immigration create an extraordinarily complex situation for any pastor who takes seriously the whole person and therefore the educational, economic, legal, cultural, and spiritual dimensions of the immigrant experience.

El Paso/Juárez is a classic example of the increasingly changing reality of the United States along the border, what *Time* magazine referred to in its 2001 special report as "amexica." As one pastor from El Paso put it, "If it were not for the river, the barbed wire fences, and the white and green Border Patrol vehicles, it would be impossible to tell where one country ends and the other begins." All of the pastors we talked to in El Paso, therefore, are challenged in different ways to help their congregations, in the words of Cliff Warner, "think and act beyond politically imposed barriers to work together for the common good."

Urban pastors in El Paso, as in so many other cities, struggle to discern how best to minister to and provide advocacy and accompaniment for immigrants, many of whom are in limbo with regard to their naturalization status and who daily experience fear and trauma. Neighborhoods and congregations can become fragmented and broken over immigration politics. In a metropolitan area that is greatly affected by the lack of basic human necessities such as medical attention, clean water, affordable and safe housing, educational opportunities, and other basic social infrastructures, should undocumented immigrants receive the benefits of citizenship? If they contribute so much to the local economy, taking jobs at wages most Americans would never accept, why should they not? What services should the church offer, and should congregations make distinctions based on naturalization status?

Immersed not only in immigrant populations but in immigration politics, pastors in border cities like El Paso, Phoenix, or San Diego see on a daily basis the future of most cities in the United States. Problems of identity concerning music and cultural aesthetics have already been mentioned as areas of challenge in urban churches. But other questions surface such as what it means to show hospitality or to provide a sense of "home" to immigrant families with a high degree of transience, who often find themselves moving, whether to afford the cheapest rent or because of eviction. Questions of how to reconcile religious conscience with what is lawful are also critical for urban pastors. What do you do, for example, when you have undocumented immigrants and Border Patrol agents attending the same church, sitting perhaps on the same pews?

One further implication of ethnic and racial diversity repeatedly mentioned by urban pastors is the increasingly widespread phenomenon of congregations sharing their space with other ethnic minority or immigrant congregations. Not only does this raise again the aforementioned question of "identity" across congregational, denominational, ethnic, racial, and theological lines, but pastors in these congregations frequently find themselves in the unenviable position of being landlords to other congregations and of mediating disputes between congregations. There arises, moreover, the question of what to do with a changing church population that pushes the envelope on mission and loses others in the process. Rose Mary Sanchez-Guzman from El Paso told us the story of how her fledgling congregation lost the space they were renting from a sister congregation in the neighborhood who had come to see them as tenants, while she and her congregation had thought all along that theirs was a partnership. Many congregations want to partner with other ethnic or language-based groups in creating multicultural models of shared ministry and resources until, for example, the English-speaking congregation finds itself smelling Korean kim-chee wafting up from the fellowship hall Sunday after Sunday during their 11 a.m. worship service. Or congregations may believe in the importance of incubating ministries of outreach to underserved populations until, for example, the ministry successfully begins to attract a throng of children who are *not* the children of the host congregation and whose activities (perceived as unruly) begin to take a toll on facility upkeep. How quickly urban partnerships can turn into tenant situations.

Despite the many challenges associated with the extraordinary diversity and transience that characterize urban life—questions, for example, such as how a pastor or congregation ministers to persons in the context of interracial marriages, relationships, and children—excellent urban pastors, or so we have found, have a profound vision of the church as a "new creation" and are capable of inspiring that vision in others. When listening to them, you often hear particular themes related to multicultural life, such as being a family or living as if we are all children of God; metaphors like tapestry, quilt, or rainbow; and passages from Scripture such as Revelation 7, where the church is presented as having been gathered out of all tribes, tongues, and nations. As T. Allen Bethel of Portland told us, "I believe the survival of the church, not in terms of ethnic constituency, but in terms of reaching souls for the Kingdom, will be predicated upon our realizing, equipping, and ministering to the whole city and all her residents. We can no longer continue to have homogenous churches identified by ethnicity alone. What a great challenge when we begin to grasp and help fulfill the great desire of Jesus that we all be one."

DIVISION AND ALIENATION

Closely related to diversity and in many ways a product of it is the tragic reality of division, fragmentation, and alienation not only throughout the city in relation to political, economic, and racial lines but also among clergy and their congregations. Of the ninety-six pastors participating in our project, one-fourth suggested the topic of "clergy divides" as the focus of their group's six-month study and reflection, with the hope that their partnerships could be models if not catalysts of healing and unity across ethnic, social, theological, and denominational lines.

The types of divides urban pastors experience vary from city to city. Sexism in the church creates one type of divide characterized by dual standards and a "stained-glass ceiling" where men are promoted to positions at more affluent churches while the urban ministry work that women do is often demeaned. As our pastors from San Diego noted, "The vision for girls in the church is tainted, skewed, and unsure. They are not encouraged to be word-bearers and leaders, but merely hearers and followers." There were yet other kinds of division and isolation that were noted—for example, that which stemmed from (what for Christian pastors is) the unusual position of being a religious minority, as in the case of our pastors from Salt Lake City. In a city that is dominated by the Mormon faith "in everything from politics, to school systems, to cultural identity," pastors experience what our Salt Lake City participants described as "a visceral dynamic of us and them, insider and outsider."

Though the pluralism of cities could serve as a context for collaboration and cooperation and a cause for celebration among pastors, too often it provides the occasion for competition and alienation based on a lack of mutual understanding born of fear and distancing. What cooperation does exist frequently takes the form of "I'll support your event if you'll support mine." Among pastors, many of the key differences are theological and ethical. As Elaine Peresluha, a pastor in Bangor, Maine, describes it, these differences result in "duplicate efforts, rivalries, and animosity keeping us from being models of respect and tolerance." Thus, for example, in Bangor, the clergy group grew in theological diversity to include rabbis and non-Christian ministers, women as well as men, until eventually the level of diversity had reached a point where the group began to fragment. The participation of a priestess of the Feminine Divine was viewed by some as the last straw, and the group eventually dissolved. One of the tragic consequences of this fragmentation, as in so many cities, is the duplication of food pantries and other forms of direct assistance from church to church with no central distribution or coordination of efforts to get food to people on a regularly scheduled basis.

Local governments often end up preying on grassroots divisions, whether intentionally or not, by pitting groups one against the other in the pursuit of limited resources for their communities. In this way, urban social policy reflects the practice of what Paulo Freire called "*dividing in order to rule.*"[19] Not only that, but as Ronald Peters notes, by concentrating on difference and uniqueness between groups, we end up entrenching our fear of the other: "After noting how others are 'different' from ourselves, . . . we assign to their dissimilarity an oppositional label that codifies their difference (and emotional distance). In other words, we objectify them, reducing their status from human beings to an assigned label or stereotype to which our fear is attached."[20] The distance and alienation created by this objectification and lack of relationship may finally manifest itself in hostility and violence.

Even though pastors tend to group with others like themselves, and even though this can contribute to a situation of polarization over ethical issues such as abortion, homosexuality, or the U.S. involvement in war, we discovered that there remains a deep hunger in pastors for moving beyond opposi-tional postures that inevitably breed fear and alienation toward models of collaboration, unity in diversity, and working together toward a common good. No wonder so many urban ministers identify reconciliation as a guiding aim of their work and a key theme for interpreting their ministry.

RESOURCES

Pastors often spoke of the urban context as a setting where the needs are many and the resources few. Indeed, for many pas-tors, pastoring in the city can feel like being asked to make "bricks without straw."[21] Of course, there are certainly areas of almost any city characterized by affluence and abundance. But it is impossible to deny the impact on the city of the economic shifts of the last several decades as U.S. cities have seen hun-dreds of thousands of industrial jobs disappear, move elsewhere, or convert into fewer, more highly professionalized positions requiring advanced education and experience. Lott's assess-ment, in fact, was echoed by many of the pastors with whom we spoke. The pay is often poor in urban situations, and it is difficult to find funding for facilities, ministries, and staff. Lim-itations in space can also prove to be a challenge in the urban context—and not simply because of the closer proximity of buildings, the lack of parking, and the density of the popula-tion. Just as with the seating in older cars, older ballparks, and even aircraft from a bygone era, older urban churches were built for a population that had nothing like the expectations we today have in terms of legroom or the physical space between persons. Older churches suffer from the often unnoticed trend that, as Lyle Schaller points out, "More space is required today to accommodate the same number of churchgoers than was needed in 1950."[22]

But beyond the economic and spatial pressures that come with urban ministry, as Jackson Carroll notes in *God's Potters*, urban pastors report spending more time than their rural counterparts in all areas of pastoral work and twice as much in administrative tasks. The workweek of the urban pastor is also 20 percent longer than that of rural pastors.[23] The intensity and stress of urban life, as well as the strain of securing adequate resources to realize a church's vision, can contribute greatly to pastoral burnout. Excellence in urban ministry, or so we have learned, is sustained by creative methods of partnering, networking, and building on otherwise undervalued resources.

After studying the way well-intended people seek solutions to the tremendous needs of the city, John Kretzmann and John McKnight, researchers at Northwestern University, noted two divergent paths. The first and by far most traveled path focuses on a community's "needs, deficiencies and problems" while the second is committed to "discovering a community's capacities and assets."[24] The first (a "needs-based" approach) cultivates in persons and communities a belief that their needs can only be met by those outside the community so that "their well-being depends upon being a client" and they come to "think of themselves and their neighbors as fundamentally deficient, victims incapable of taking charge of their lives and of their community's future." Urban ministers who follow this path focus on providing services to meet perceived needs and busy themselves in the quest for outside funding and resources. The second path, by contrast (an "asset-based" approach)—and this we would identify as a mark of excellence among urban pastors— recognizes that one of the keys to urban transformation is "to locate all of the available local assets, to begin connecting them with one another in ways that multiply their power and effectiveness, and to begin harnessing those local institutions that are not yet available for local development purposes."[25] Examples of local institutions with whom the urban pastors we studied found partnership ranged from colleges and universities and dance troupes to senior citizens groups and merchant associations. In a needs-based approach, institutions and associations such as these would never appear on the "map." From the standpoint of an asset-based approach, however, "even the poorest neighborhood is a place where individuals and organizations represent resources upon which to rebuild."[26]

Whether through multiple usage of space, congregational bridging, student volunteers, or even the pooling of a women's group's funds by one of our San Diego pastors to purchase and divide half a cow so that everyone had more than enough (with apologies to vegetarians), excellent urban pastors reinforce the observation by Kretzmann and McKnight that "communities are never built from the top down, or from the outside in."[27] Rather, when resources are scarce, the creativity and ingenuity of the people of God, born out of prayer, partnership, and trust in the Spirit of God who is liberal in giving gifts, communities are restored from the bottom of communities upward and from the inside of communities outward. As one pastor suggested at our project's concluding conference, "Nothing can be done without networking. In the beginning, even God said, "Let *us* . . ."

2

Cultivating Holy Friendships

> Bear one another's burdens, and in this way you will fulfill the
> law of Christ.
>
> (Gal. 6:2)

Aristotle once said, "No one would choose to live without friends even if he had all the other goods."[1] That is undoubtedly true, and especially so in the context of urban pastoral ministry where partnership and friendship are both a defining quality of pastoral excellence and a means toward sustaining it. Pastoring can be lonely—even in the city where, ironically, one is likely to rub shoulders with dozens of other people all day long. As Anna Olson, a pastor from Los Angeles told us, "Our urban life is tremendously fast-paced and often isolating. It is easy to believe that we alone are coping with the problems we face." Despite multiple interactions with numerous people on a daily basis, whether in the context of congregational life or in the course of normal urban life, pastors can become isolated and alienated without the close companionship of peers. They may experience what Howard Thurman spoke of as "contact without fellowship," contact that is "devoid of any of the primary overtures of warmth and fellow-feeling and genuineness."[2]

In a study of the physical and emotional health of pastors conducted by the Pulpit and Pew project,[3] many of the top thir-

teen factors identified by pastors as associated with their health
and job satisfaction, including all four of the leading factors,
relate to loneliness, relationships, and difficulties in cultivating
life-giving friendships:

1. Feeling lonely and isolated
2. Difficulty having private life apart from clergy role
3. Perceiving different treatment as clergy
4. Lack of agreement over clergy role
5. Congregation making too many demands
6. Stress from congregation's challenges
7. Congregation critical of pastor
8. Stress from congregation's criticisms
9. Feeling loved and cared for by congregation
10. Little time for recreation, relaxation, reflection
11. Work preventing time with children
12. Spouse resenting time ministry takes
13. Spouse resenting financial situation[4]

Clearly, cultivating friendships does not come naturally for
many pastors. Within congregations and denominational bodies, there persists a culture of emphasizing the individual
accomplishments of the pastor while ignoring the importance
of mutual encouragement or the sense in which pastoral excellence is a shared excellence, the product of mutual support and
encouragement. Pastors may come to be complicit in these
expectations, hiding their weaknesses, guarding their public
image, and denying their needs for the friendship of others. A
pastor's spouse often suffers alongside the pastor in this
regard—if not more so. And even though both pastor and
spouse may be formally admired, respected, and even cele-
brated by the congregation, a silence often develops around the
need for pastoral support and friendship lest someone find
chinks in the armor. It becomes particularly difficult for pastors
to develop close personal friendships when they are put on a
pedestal or held to higher moral standards than the rest of the
congregation. Add to all of this the wider society's emphasis on

rugged individualism and personal achievement, and you have a surefire recipe for pastoral loneliness and isolation.

But there are even more important and complicated reasons for pastoral loneliness and for the lack of friendships that sustain pastoral excellence. How pastors relate to their parishioners is an extraordinarily sensitive matter related to the larger question of professional boundaries and roles. Pastors are frequently advised by their denominations and by fellow pastors to avoid developing friendships with their parishioners. For one thing, pastors are often privy to information about their parishioners gained in the context of pastoral counseling. Some of this information pertains to problems parishioners might be having with family, money, sexuality, gambling, marital infidelities, or job-related difficulties. Parishioners will not likely feel confident trusting their pastor with such information if they know the pastor is a close friend with others in the congregation with whom he or she might share that information. Then, too, there is the perception of favoritism and the potential of close pastoral friendships developing into inappropriate sexual relationships.[5] On top of all this, a pastor may often need to serve as the prophetic voice within the church community, and the question naturally arises as to the distance a pastor should maintain so as to be able to speak boldly and without softening the prophetic word where close friendships are at stake.

All of these concerns are legitimate and important, though complex. Some of them, however, may presuppose understandings of friendship that are not necessarily Christian—as, for example, a supposition that being prophetic to others may require that we not be their close friends. In addressing these concerns, at least one way of moving forward is to consider carefully the nature of friendship in the context of the *church*. If Aristotle was correct that friendship is essential to the good life, then the kind of friendship we value depends entirely on what we understand the good life to be. Our formation into the good life and into the virtues, or patterns of excellence that constitute the good life, always requires a social context in which excellence can be recognized and the kinds of friendships in which that excellence can be cultivated. For the Christian (unlike Aristotle), that social context is, of course, the body of Christ. Friendship within the body of Christ, while it may resemble other types of friendship, is nonetheless distinctive. It would not be wrong to describe the church as a community of friends.

The theological dimensions of friendship are significant here, and they take us beyond Aristotle's more formal observations about the relationship of friendship to excellence, or virtue. For the friendships we cultivate within the body of Christ find their origin, substance, and integrity in our relationship to Christ who has called us his "friends" (John 15:15). Our friendship with Christ, in other words, provides the paradigm and framework for our friendships with one another within the body of Christ.

If friendship with Christ is the starting point for understanding Christian friendship, then one of the first things we learn is that this friendship is not an intimacy that is merely sentimental or cozy, characterized by overattachment to those who either like us or are like us. On the contrary, Christian friendship is risky and challenging, and requires a vulnerability premised on mutual commitment and expectation that involves the possibility our friends may change us. Before warning his disciples that the world would hate them because they did not belong to it, Christ sent them into the world with the commandment to love one another. But in thus sending and commissioning the disciples, he claimed that the obedience he sought from them was that of *friends* rather than *servants*. They were not merely to follow orders but instead they had been made participants with Christ in the mission on which he himself had been sent.

"As his friends," so David Burrell points out, "we are liberated from having to prove ourselves by accomplishing great deeds. We are already accepted as intimates."[6] The ministry we have been given by Christ in the context of friendship, therefore, can be carried out with patience and joy, making room for the unexpected, rather than with obligation and a tyrannizing sense that the results of ministry are ours to predict and control.

Christ calls his friends to bear fruit, to be sure, but from a posture of trust rather than compulsion. At the same time, as Burrell continues, "we are not dispensed from the response characteristic of friendship: to become what the other's trust would call forth from us."

When excellence is defined in terms of spiritual practice, virtuous character, and nurturing relationships rather than in terms of doing more or knowing more, then there is an important sense in which friendship is at the core of pastoral excellence rather than being merely external or instrumental to it. In other words, we do not start out, as Paul Wadell warns, as "fully formed individuals for whom intimate relationships are arbitrary possibilities." On the contrary, "we grow into true individuality and personhood only in and through relationships with others."[7] Friendships, then, are not simply a means of supporting a more healthy spiritual life. As some of the pastors in our project put it, "They *are* our spiritual life." For this reason, pastoral friendships may be described as nothing short of "holy."

Gregory Jones and Kevin Armstrong have suggested that friendships are "holy" in at least two important ways. First, they are holy when they are "oriented toward discernment and deepening of Christian vocation, as well as nurturing growth in the Christian life, toward our learning how to live as holy people." The point here is not that these friends are already holy and then transfer that holiness to us by our association with them. Rather, "Holy friends are our companions on the journey of learning to desire and love God truly and faithfully."[8]

Often a spouse or a close loved one can serve as a friend and an agent of hope and support on this journey and in the midst of pastoral loneliness. But what we have learned from our work with the urban pastors who formed four-person partnerships as the basis for their spiritual renewal is that there is no substitute for the friendship of other pastors—fellow travelers who can share vulnerabilities, insights, and experiences while forgoing the posturing and competition that too often characterize clergy associations or denominational gatherings. Erin Gilmore, a pastor in Salt Lake City, put it this way: "For the first time since moving to Utah I feel like I have found a group with whom I can be myself without fear or caution. I have been a part of several clergy groups here in Utah, but they all have had a particular issue or reason for gathering. . . . When you do not feel as alone, and when you do not have to hold everything inside, but have a place to let down your guard, and be honest and real within a safe community, the pressure and responsibility of ministry doesn't disappear, but it is not as heavy somehow."

One of the most frequently mentioned features of the friendships developed through the vehicle of pastoral partnerships was their role in providing a place where pastors could be "human beings" again. Mike Woods of El Paso told us the partnerships "helped to counteract the depersonalizing tendencies of urban pastoral ministry," while Wellesley Ferguson of New York described his participation as an opportunity to "cast off some of the 'clergy thing.'" Others spoke about being able to be open and free to be themselves, especially among other clergy, without being judged for being stressed or bogged down. No wonder joy was a recurring theme in our pastors' descriptions of their partnerships and of finding the opportunity to share their passions, concerns, and struggles—or even being able to vent and to share horror stories about their experience in urban ministry. Pastoral partnerships were described not as energy-draining, but as life-giving. As Gilmore said, "In an urban environment there are hundreds of groups and causes and issues and I can give away all my time to different clergy groups, or community organizations, but none of those ultimately are going to ask me how I am doing." It is easy to see why the pastors described their partnerships as "safe space," "sanctuary," and "a place of trust."

Again, it is trust rather than compulsion that characterizes both our expectations of and our responses to those whom we count as friends. Communities of friendship form us into patterns of excellence through mutual affection and the bearing of burdens but also by providing us accountability for the exercise of the disciplines necessary for spiritual, emotional, intellectual, and physical renewal. As Paul Wadell says in his book *Becoming Friends*, "Every friendship is an adventure, a journey perhaps, that changes us over time, shaping our character, forming our habits, cultivating in us attitudes and dispositions that stand as an inventory of the relationships we have had and the effect they have had on us."[9]

Holy friends are those who do not take advantage of our vulnerabilities, attempting to control or manipulate us, on the one hand, nor do they merely tell us what we want to hear, on the other hand. We are obliged and indebted to holy friends, but we also experience them as liberating us to be ourselves. They give us perspective on God's Spirit at work in our lives and then support and encourage us to open ourselves to the Spirit. "Holy friends," as Jones and Armstrong suggest, "are those who, over time, get to know us well enough that they can challenge sins we have come to love, affirm gifts we are afraid to claim, and dream dreams about how we can bear witness to God's kingdom that we otherwise would not have dreamed."[10]

If, in the first place, friendships are holy because they deepen Christian vocation, nurture growth in the Christian life, and form us into a holy people, they are holy, secondly, because they arise out of a common connection to the source of all holiness in a way that transcends—by way of including rather than ignoring—racial, ethnic, gender, ideological, and socioeconomic diversity. As Jones and Armstrong put it, "These relationships are often unlikely to be developed apart from a mutual attraction to the gospel life. They bring people together from different backgrounds and histories, with diverse hopes and fears."[11]

Because holy friendships strike this balance between unity and diversity, cultivating them is a practice that is more like a skill, or perhaps an art—it does not come naturally but must be learned. It is not just a matter of snuggling up to those who are closest to us. It is true, of course, that friendship produces a degree of sameness. In his *Confessions*, for instance, Augustine claims, "There can be no true friendship unless those who cling to each other are welded together by you [God] in that love which is spread throughout our hearts by the holy spirit which is given to us."[12] He goes on to describe the company of friends as follows:

> . . . to talk and laugh and do kindnesses to each other; to read pleasant books together; to make jokes together and then talk seriously together; sometimes to disagree, but without any ill feeling, just as one may disagree with oneself, and to find that these very rare disagreements made our general agreement all the sweeter; to be sometimes teaching and sometimes learning; to long impatiently for the absent and to welcome them with joy when they returned to us. These and other similar expressions of feeling, which proceed from the hearts of those who love and are loved in return, and are revealed in the face, the voice, the eyes, and in a thousand charming ways, were like a kindling fire to melt our souls together and out of many to make us one.[13]

At the same time, diversity and difference is important in friendship, precisely because of the way it challenges us to dream new dreams, cast off favorite sins, and claim gifts we are afraid to claim. People who are too similar are not likely to be able to do this, and indeed, as Jones and Armstrong note, "we need the presence of [diverse] others to keep us from self-deception, to remind us when our sins are masking as virtues or our tolerance is being used to isolate rather than welcome others."[14] Many of the more significant pastoral partnerships we watched develop during the course of our project were ecumenical in nature, transcending their own intra-denominational concerns and affording each other new perspectives on pastoral life and ministry.

Likewise, the pastoral partnerships where we saw holy friendships develop were those where the pastors liked each other and enjoyed spending time in each other's company, to be sure, but these friendships were not cliquish nor did they have the effect of shutting the pastors off to other friendships.[15] As Wadell says, "True friendships should always make our world bigger, not smaller, by encouraging us to see everyone more compassionately and magnanimously. Friendships are corrupted—indeed, they become morally and spiritually dangerous—when their effect is to leave us ignoring the neighbors Jesus calls us to love."[16] It could even be, though we were not able to measure this, that the cultivation of key pastoral friendships is a practice that can support and lead to the practice of pastors becoming better friends with their own parishioners, even admitting the complexity and the importance of appropriate boundaries, conversational limits, and confidentiality.

FRIENDSHIP AND BOWLS

One group of pastors from Bangor, Maine, formed friendship around the metaphor—and the reality—of bowls. They decided that pastors need to do more than merely meet together to discuss theological and social issues. So they engaged in art—in particular, the making of bowls. "We have found solace in one another not through conversation only but through doing art together; through meeting around a table with paper and wallpaper paste and painting and clay. Indeed we have found that as our imaginations and hands have been opened to the materials in front of us, so too our hearts have been opened to listening to one another more intentionally and intently. This finding of common ground through the doing of art has provided us with a metaphor, a dream, a plan." The pastors were from United Church of Christ, Unitarian-Universalist, United Methodist, and Lutheran traditions.

It may be no surprise that all four of the pastors from Bangor were women who had no vested interest in maintaining the more formal, linear, and hierarchical meeting patterns established by male-dominated clergy associations. Most of us know instinctively that true friendship takes time and patience. The commitment, risk, and challenge of friendship is such that we become "more adept at isolation and loneliness than we are at intimacy and friendship."[17] But the Bangor pastors took that risk and, as they put it, began to see themselves not only as creating bowls but being bowls—"containers that could hold the bruised and bleeding, minister to the conflicts and hold all the diversity amongst us, with faith."

The use of art in forming pastoral friendships or the use of other less controlled media and venues may be more important than it might at first seem. True friendships require a degree of playfulness and humor. Art, like play (or art *as* play) leaves us vulnerable; in playing we often reveal ourselves. "Playfulness is a sign not only that people are comfortable with one another but also that they are not afraid to be themselves with one another. Playfulness allows the masks and facades to melt away and a kind of 'epiphany in silliness' to occur where people reveal themselves more honestly and completely to one another."[18] With a fair amount of certainty, we can report that we have not seen pastoral partnerships develop into authentic friendships where there has not been a healthy level of play. This is yet another of the good reasons, by the way, why eating together has also proved to be crucial for pastors in their partnering together.

The pastors from Bangor, we think, have a lot to teach clergy and the way they go about relating to one another. In their words,

> The dream is to offer the same opportunity to other ministers and parishioners as well—an invitation for folks in our congregations and other ministers to gather with art to create—not for the sake of talking about Iraq or homosexuality or the meaning of Jesus' suffering but for the sake of plain old listening, of just getting to know one another. It is a modest beginning but we believe it is the only hope we have for offering a way through the quagmire of polarization and defensiveness that now infects us all. Just maybe, after folk have cut and pasted and painted and imagined and laughed and talked about the crazy Maine weather and the challenges of raising children these days, they might be willing to talk of other things. Who knows?

THE POINT OF FRIENDSHIP

As valuable as friendship is for sustaining pastoral excellence and, indeed, for helping us learn what excellence is in the first place and then transforming us into the kinds of people God calls us to be, a caveat may be in order in speaking in terms of the value of friendship. This caveat relates to the difficulty of sustaining friendships in a consumer culture where value is determined instrumentally. To reiterate what urban pastors have told us, friendships are not simply a means of supporting a more healthy spiritual life, they *are* the spiritual life, or at least central to it. The logic of consumerism emphasizes choice so that even our relationships with others are pursued within a calculus of costs and benefits. Even Aristotle realized this when he distinguished between three types of friendship corresponding to the three objects of love—those that give us *pleasure*, those that are *useful* to us, and those that are based on *virtue*.

> Those who love each other for utility love the other not in his own right, but insofar as they gain some good for themselves from him. The same is true of those who love for pleasure; for they like a witty person not because of his character, but because he is pleasant to them. . . . Hence these friendships as well [as the friends] are coincidental, since the beloved is loved not insofar as he is who he is, but insofar as he provides some good or pleasure. And so these sorts of friendships are easily dissolved, when the friends do not remain similar [to what they were]; for if someone is no longer pleasant or useful, the other stops loving him.[19]

While holy friendships are good for us, they are not to be valued primarily because they are advantageous to us. To place friendships within a utilitarian or consumerist framework inevitably trivializes them, leading us to abandon them when they do not serve some external purpose. A holy friendship is, on the contrary, a form of commitment and a willingness to be available even when we do not stand to benefit in some clear or immediate way. Again, Aristotle grasps this important distinction in describing a "complete" or "perfect" friendship as

> the friendship of good people similar in virtue; for they wish goods in the same way to each other insofar as they are good, and they are good in their own right. Now those who wish goods to their friends for the friend's own sake are friends most of all; for they have this attitude because of the friend himself, not coincidentally. Hence these people's friendship lasts as long as they are good; and virtue is enduring.[20]

Christians, of course, know that the source of all goodness including their own is God and that good friendships endure and are sustained by friendship with God. But in a culture where we are always on the move and find it difficult to get to know others deeply, where we lack the patience and presence required for friendship, where we tend to value everything, including friendship, in market categories in terms of "exchange" value, we do well to remember that excellence (virtue) "begins and ends in friendship."[21]

3

Sabbath Practices: Creation and Liberation

So God blessed the seventh day and hallowed it, because on it
God rested from all the work that he had done in creation.
(Gen. 2:3)

When Constance Wells saw the wide-open spaces of the Arizona desert, she realized how tired she was. A United Church
of Christ pastor from Bangor, Maine, Connie spent part of her
sabbatical in the Southwest. She described the experience:
"Being touched by the timeless winds of Arizona was like living
in the presence of the deep, wide, constant and embracing Holy
Spirit. The space of it gave me appreciation for God's creating,
loving presence in all creation. . . . The most amazing part for
me was daring, trusting once again, to open myself to that God
presence. I realized how wary, weary, and shut down one can
become in urban pastoral ministry." It was an experience of
being apart, away from her usual contexts of ministry, from the
city, from the usual patterns that kept her from herself and from
God's presence. It was a time of rest and freedom and re-
creation—a Sabbath.

In the initial stages of the Sustaining Urban Pastoral Excellence project, we called the four to eight weeks of time off from
ministry a paid "enrichment leave." Pastors could take time apart
from their congregations to travel, participate in a retreat, attend
a conference, broaden their horizons, get fresh perspective, rest,

and come back renewed for ministry. Within the first year, we changed our language to that of sabbatical and, increasingly, to the root of that word: "Sabbath." Sabbath provided a powerful theological framework—missing in the term "enrichment leave"—for pastors to consider the meaning of their work, their need for rest, and the ground of their vocation. It enabled pastors to see the time away not as vacation but as a practice of spiritual renewal deeply embedded in Jewish and Christian tradition. For some pastors the language of Sabbath was unfamiliar; others had maintained Sabbath practices for years. Almost all found Sabbath to be a great gift offering badly needed rest and balance, opening up a different way of being, helping to restore right relationships with self, family, and community. Cultivating practices of Sabbath keeping proved to be renewing and transformative for urban pastors; indeed, some described these practices as "life-changing."

The process of developing Sabbath practices, however, was also challenging for some urban pastors, and those more difficult experiences also shed light on urban ministry and spirituality in contemporary culture. Some found sabbatical to be too abrupt a shift from their usual habits of work (in their words, "workaholism"). Some felt adrift without their identity as pastor. Others struggled to negotiate boundaries with congregations. And while pastors' sabbaticals often yielded newly empowered lay leadership within the congregation, pastors did not always find it a smooth transition back to the pulpit.

The experiences of urban pastors in our program point to the importance of cultivating practices of Sabbath keeping early in the formation for ministry, supporting periodic sabbaticals for pastors throughout their ministry, and developing congregational ecologies that nurture Sabbath practices among laity and clergy. We also saw how very countercultural is the practice of Sabbath keeping, how pastors' identities and understandings of success—and the expectations that their congregations place on them—are bound up with productivity and immediate usefulness. Too often pastors described Sabbath in instrumental terms as a tool to increase their effectiveness and efficiency. We would resist that utilitarian sense of Sabbath—common as it might be. Practices of Sabbath keeping are indeed foundational to ministry. Yet this is so not because Sabbath keeping is a self-help tool or leadership strategy; rather, it is a practice that embodies and rediscovers right understanding of God as creator, our own identity as created beings, and the gift of freedom from unceasing work.

CREATION AND LIBERATION: UNDERSTANDINGS OF SABBATH IN THE TRADITION

The history of Sabbath practice and interpretation is quite complex. Sabbath keeping often is considered to be the central practice of Judaism, the mark of Jewish identity, and even the preserver of the Jewish people amidst the loss of the temple. Interpretations of Sabbath in both Judaism and Christianity, however, vary widely.[1] Theologians and biblical scholars have long debated issues such as how to interpret rules for correct Sabbath observance, whether the Sabbath was intended for all or just for the Israelites, the relationship between law and gospel, and the meaning of the Sabbath for Christians. We will not be able to explore these complex debates here, but we can identify some important frameworks for understanding practices of Sabbath keeping.

Two themes emerge as central motifs—creation and liberation. The first emphasizes Sabbath as a time of awed respect for God as creator and for the wonder of the created world, an imitation of the divine rhythm of creation and rest, work and Sabbath. Biblical texts clearly link Sabbath to the creation story: "So God blessed the seventh day and hallowed it, because on it God rested from all the work that he had done in creation" (Gen. 2:3). Passages in Exodus link the Sabbath command to the creation story and God's sanctification of the seventh day. In Exodus 20, the Lord God speaks from Mount Sinai to the Israelite people: "Remember the sabbath day, and keep it holy. Six days you shall labor and do all your work. But the seventh day is a sabbath to the Lord your God; you shall not do any work" (8–10). The rationale for the Sabbath stems from the creation story: "For in six days the Lord made heaven and earth, the sea, and all that is in them, but rested the seventh day; therefore the Lord blessed the sabbath day and consecrated it" (Exod. 20:11). There is a clear connection between Sabbath and God's creative activity. As Judaic scholar Elliot Ginsburg writes: "The sabbath is both the crown of God's creation and the climax of each mundane week."[2] It needs no instrumental or human-centered rationale.

The second theme emphasizes the liberative gift of Sabbath. Sabbath observance recalls Yahweh's liberation of the Jewish people from slavery: "Observe the sabbath day and keep it holy, as the Lord your God commanded you. . . . Remember that you were a slave in the land of Egypt, and the Lord your God brought you out from there with a mighty hand and an outstretched arm; therefore the Lord your God commanded you to keep the sabbath day" (Deut. 5:12, 15). Sabbath keeping continues to free people from slavery, drudgery, technology, and consumerism. Exodus 20:10 extends the Sabbath command to the entire household, including slaves and animals, as well as resident aliens of the town. Sabbath represents freedom and justice for all creation, recognition of the dignity of all created beings. Jewish theologian Abraham Joshua Heschel writes: "The seventh day is the exodus from tension, the liberation of man from his own muddiness, the installation of man as a sovereign in the world of time."[3] It should be noted here that the passages from Exodus and Deuteronomy clearly describe Sabbath as a command (not an option), though a liberative one.[4]

The treatment of Sabbath in the Gospels of Matthew and Mark reinforce a liberating understanding of Sabbath and portray Jesus as a fairly liberal interpreter of the Sabbath command. When the Pharisees chastise his hungry disciples for picking grain on the Sabbath, Jesus responds: "The sabbath was made for humankind, and not humankind for the sabbath; so the Son of Man is lord even of the sabbath" (Mark 2:27–28). When he heals a man with a withered hand in the synagogue on the

Sabbath, Jesus justifies his action with this guideline: "It is law-ful to do good on the sabbath" (Matt. 12:12).

Some see a tension in these two motifs, with the first being more theocentric and the second more humanistic. Urban pas-tors' experiences of sabbatical, however, suggest that practices of Sabbath keeping can embody both motifs. Sabbath practices are humanizing, offering much-needed rest and freedom from unhealthy, even idolatrous, patterns of work and life. They offer a framework for self-care but are far from pop forms of self-help. As people pause and rest, they become more spacious, more attentive to and grateful for the gifts of creation. They often deepen their connection to the natural world and find delight in the creative process. Sabbath practice points one to the Creator and opens doors to wonder, freedom, and play.

A CALL TO REST

Urban pastors are drawn to the command to rest. They par-ticularly appreciate having a religious rationale for rest because many feel that they need "permission" to take time apart from ministry. Indeed, sabbatical and other Sabbath practices are an important corrective to the exhaustion, burnout, over-functioning, and even trauma experienced by many urban pastors. Sabbatical often serves as liberation from habits of overwork and as an invitation to self-care. At the same time, the call to rest competes against strong cultural pressures toward productivity.

Undoubtedly, rest is not a need unique to urban pastors. Laypersons as well as pastors in rural and suburban contexts also struggle with the rapid pace of living, multiple demands, work pressures, and family responsibilities. Still, as we have shown in chapter 1, the urban context poses distinctive chal-lenges that make Sabbath practices both particularly difficult and particularly compelling. Wes Philips of El Paso noted: "The urban environment is too rushed and our people don't know how to rest." Several pastors spoke about serious burnout caused by long work hours and the ceaseless demands of urban ministry. They described being "exhausted in every way," "addicted to busy," "over-functioning," and "workaholic." They lamented having no space for reflection or even "catching my breath." One pastor said that she "had not realized how uncivilized my life had become. My life often felt like drudgery."

Both ministry and the urban environment reward productivity—the combination for urban pastors can be dangerous. According to Lewis Nicholson of Hampton Roads, Virginia, "We wear our exhaustion as a trophy; [saying] 'real character is being able to handle stress.' And the self-indulged busyness makes us appear and feel important." Lorraine Anderson of Boston recalled what she was like before the sabbatical: "I think I am never going to go back, by God's grace, to that pace that I was living at before. Sort of driven, too driven, kind of on the edge." Through an intentional practice of Sabbath keeping, beginning on Saturday evening and extending through Sunday ("because I want the church to observe the Sabbath"), Anderson learned "to be present to the moment. . . . I am doing less and deeper rather than more and more frazzled."

It took some time, though, for pastors to learn the art of doing less. Sabbath can come as a rather foreign and uncomfortable intrusion for those accustomed to busyness. Many set off on sabbatical with grand projects—refinishing a basement, writing a book—and then quickly scaled back their plans as they felt fatigue hit them once they stopped working. One pastor reflected that he planned to finish writing a book but ended up sleeping *a lot*, especially when he thought about writing. When he returned from sabbatical he passed along this advice to other pastors entering the project: "Do what you do, but take care of yourself." As Chauncey Brown of Syracuse put it, some time is needed to "get away and relax and pray and not have to worry about always giving, giving, giving, but taking some time to receive myself."

Sabbatical can help pastors not just care for self but even find themselves, rediscovering a sense of authenticity that can get lost in urban ministry. One pastor said that the sabbatical leave helped him to "find myself again, my spirit, my center." Cliff Warner, an Episcopal priest in El Paso, spoke about sabbatical as providing "space to remember" who one is as an individual. The leave helped in "reconnecting with who I am as an individual—apart from the congregational pressures on identity formation/perception. . . . There are aspects of who I am that are not supported by the congregation (nor are they opposed, by the way). That part of me tends to fade away unless I have space to remember."

As vital as sabbatical is, however, urban pastors sometimes feel guilty for taking time apart from ministry. Their parishioners' crises continue unabated. Their parishioners—and their spouses—do not get similar time off from work. One pastor told himself he was "just gonna rest . . . but my conscience was whuppin' me"; the next time, he said, he will know better *how* to do a sabbatical. Others wrestled with feelings of displacement, even loss of identity, as they moved out of their role as pastor. One acknowledged that she "enabled" others' demands on her time. Congregations also were not always understanding of their pastors' need for time apart; some congregations resented the pastor's absence or even felt abandoned by the pastor. Grace Bartlett of Bangor wrote: "I have come to realize that the congregation for the most part does not recognize how demanding and stressful urban ministry can be. In fact it seems that the world at large and the congregational demands work at cross-purposes to such renewal. It is countercultural to take Sabbath/sabbatical breaks in a world that values and rewards the Protestant work ethic." Clearly, strong cultural factors do indeed make sabbatical and Sabbath keeping odd practices today. This is not the case only for urban pastors, but urban pastors encounter particularly stressful demands and carry a sense of Christian vocation that elevates self-sacrifice and makes boundary setting problematic.

The pressure toward productivity and activity experienced by urban pastors is particularly problematic when it conflicts with their actual vocation—when they find themselves too busy to pray, inattentive to important relationships, exhausted and neglectful of their own health, inauthentic and frazzled. Curtis Edmonds, a pastor in Hampton Roads, Virginia, expressed this when he noted that he can "get so busy with church work, and neglect the work of the kingdom." Another pastor realized that "a lot of the time, I seem to be doing things that aren't even related to my call." When they took time apart from those patterns of work, pastors often saw their ministry in new perspective. Some even came to call their work "idolatrous" in that they left little space for God (or the laity) to work; everything depended on the pastor. Sabbath practices can lead pastors to a renewed perspective on vocation. Altagracia Pérez of Los Angeles quipped that during her sabbatical she learned that "Sabbath is my true vocation." In fact, Sabbath does point us to our authentic call, which includes dignified labor but also entails regularly pausing from all forms of work. As Heschel cautioned: "One must abstain from toil and strain on the seventh day, even from strain in the service of God."[5] This is the liberation—the gift of freedom from drudgery and even from good work.

A CALL TO CREATIVITY

In his collection of Sabbath poems, Wendell Berry writes:

> I go among trees and sit still.
> All my stirring becomes quiet
> Around me like circles on water.
> My tasks lie in their places
> where I left them, asleep like cattle.

Berry goes on to describe a process of living "for a while" in the presence of our fears, there in the stillness, until the fear leaves us and what we fear in those things leaves them, until "After days of labor, / mute in my consternations, / I hear my song at last, / and I sing it."[6]

Many urban pastors found that Sabbath time led them gradually to their own song, to rediscovery of their own being and

creativity. Elaine Hewes of Bangor noted: "Because of my sabbatical, I have begun to work on my poetry and children's books
again, and can sense a 'depth of heart and soul' that had been
getting more than a little shallow." One pastor began playing
the guitar and writing music after many years when he "had no
time for" that creative outlet. Another returned to his love of
cooking. Renewed creativity was fun and energizing. For some
it also was a deeply spiritual practice, a kind of imitation or participation in God's creative activity. Often it went hand in hand
with a connection to nature, attentive as was Berry to the small
wonders of the created world.

Some found that connection to nature and creativity in the
city. Grace Bartlett, also from Bangor, discovered a great blue
heron in a cemetery where she likes to walk. She photographed
it as it grew over the course of a summer, talking to it, building
a trust relationship—"the gift of God's creation," she says. For
her, photography is a spiritual practice that enables her to
"notice the obvious" and to "look about for God's light." She
describes her experience in the darkroom, feeding papers one
by one into the developer, never sure how the image captured
would appear, and "little by little the image starts to emerge—
that is the mysterious, the creative. . . . We are partners in the
creative process."

Craig French, from Syracuse, expressed a similar awe of the
creative process: "From nothing to something. . . . A sheet of
paper that you write a poem on. God created the universe out
of nothing and gave us the same ability to create. At the end of
the day what can I look at and say 'Wow, that's good'?" Though
not a natural artist ("Art scares the pants off me," he noted),
French did an art retreat as part of his sabbatical.

While urban pastors can find connection to nature and their
own creative spark in the city, they often seek out different landscapes during sabbatical. More expansive, quieter, and greener
locales seem quite important as Sabbath space. As Psalm 23
reads, the Lord "makes me lie down in green pastures; he leads
me beside still waters; he restores my soul." Steve Pedigo, who
ministered in the Cabrini-Green public housing complex in

Chicago, "went from the streets to the mountains, hills, ocean, and forest. It felt like the weight of the ministry was lifted off my shoulders." Bartlett brought her camera from Bangor to the Grand Canyon, where she spent five weeks of her sabbatical and wished for more. LaSandra Melton-Dolberry of San Diego made it a habit to go "far away from civilization, where creation is evident—birds, water, and quietness of nature." Not answering telephones, not opening doors, the stillness of nature would center her and then, "back to craziness." Claudia Rowe's travel from her home in Seattle, Washington, to Alaska enabled her to feel a resonance between the expanse of the natural landscape and God's expansive generosity. Echoing Connie Wells's reflections in Arizona, she said that her sabbatical "was an experience of bathing in the generosity of God and God's love." The time and the expansiveness of the space and beauty of Alaska when combined with wonderful hospitality on the part of Alaskans she met simply reinforced over and over every hour of every day how good God is.

A CALL TO WORSHIP

"How great thou art"—Sabbath is about worship. It is time to praise God and draw close in relationship with the divine. We found that urban pastors love worship but at times find it liberating to be released from the weekly responsibility of sermon preparation and worship leadership. Michael Johnson of New York City named a "blessed and joyful worship experience" as one of the practices he has found most helpful in sustaining urban pastoral excellence, for "worship is at the heart of what we do." Marlene Pedigo, a Quaker ministering in a high-violence neighborhood in Chicago, wrote: "The importance of corporate worship is the sense that as one attempts 'peacemaking' in the urban context you are not alone. There are those within the church who share the ministry. It is the reminder that God is truly aware of all circumstances and working for our good!!!" However, pastors live with the tension of constant responsibility of leading worship, which does not always permit full participation in worship. Sunday, the day of worship, the day commonly regarded as the Christian Sabbath, is an intense day of work for pastors.

One of the greatest rewards for pastors on sabbatical was the opportunity to worship in other congregations or to simply experience release from the work of worship leadership. One pastor relished freedom from the "weekly grind" of sermon preparation. Another cherished the opportunity to partake in Eucharist when she was not the celebrant. Many attended other local churches—sometimes anonymously. They found it renewing and also generative of ideas for their own congregation's worship. Debra Collins of El Paso commented: "I was also able to reflect on the wonder of worship. . . . So many times on Sunday, I am busy with people or helping with a crisis that has developed that I do not actually participate in all of the worship service with the congregation. It was nice to have five Sundays of worship without a single interruption. This leave time allowed me to focus once again on my own need for worship and reflection."

THE POWER OF PLACE: CULTIVATING SABBATH SPACE IN A VARIETY OF CONTEXTS

Sabbath space can be found in different kinds of places, but those places will shape the practice of Sabbath. Different spaces draw out stillness or busyness. They offer varied images for the spiritual experience—the mountaintop Elijah experience or the touch of Jesus among the throng, the solitary desert or the quotidian spirituality of the home. So, too, practices such as Sabbath keeping can change the kind of encounter one has with God in a certain place—patterning us according to a different rhythm, opening up different experiences of the sacred, making room for different kinds of relationships in that place.

Change of place can itself be spiritual practice, as the practice of pilgrimage exemplifies. Travel often is an important dimension of sabbatical. For urban pastors, travel creates some physical and emotional distance from the congregation. They are less likely to "swing by the office" to check on things and less available to members of the congregation. The change in context lets them detach and gain fresh perspective. Travel also can be a good way to reconnect with family and friends. Some pastors went on retreats. Many appreciated the opportunity to enjoy travel time with spouses, which they described as enriching to their marriages. Some returned to native homelands, for example, to Bolivia or Jamaica. Many pastors reported that sabbatical travel was refreshing and enjoyable, although Jed Mannis, a pastor from Boston, noted that his overly ambitious trip to London turned out to be exhausting. Removed from their normal contexts of work and home, pastors generally were more relaxed, reflective, and relational, more open to new ways of being. And they were less likely to be preoccupied with life at the congregation.

For some, travel also was a kind of transformative pilgrimage. Boston pastor Karen Fritz spent five of her eight weeks in Ghana, West Africa. She stayed for some time at a retreat center and spent time with her congregation's sister congregation in Hoeviefe. She also traveled on her own around the country. She found that living in a different culture helped her to "live in the moment and take life as it comes since I had very little control on its flow." The very different culture prompted her to question her own culture's assumptions and to live more slowly and attentively: "I found the space to take the temperature of my own emotions and notice my own stresses and hungers. . . . Without the pace that I often accept from technology, I found I could hear birds and goats and the sounds of village life in new ways. With so many languages spoken in Ghana I often had to "listen hard" in order to understand without words." She came away not only personally transformed but with a different vision of church: "In West Africa, I saw the church in a new light as people danced and drummed to an ancient pulse and ministered in such prophetic ways regarding issues of trauma."

Sometimes a change of place is needed for inner transformation, or simply for prayer and rest. In the Gospel of Mark, Jesus tells his weary apostles to "'come away to a deserted place all by yourselves and rest a while.' For many were coming and going and they had no leisure even to eat" (Mark 6:31). Urban pastors find comfort in that call, and many respond eagerly when given a chance. Steve Reinhard of Salt Lake City, for example, spent thirty days in solitude on a mountain in Colorado. Joan Murray from Boston completed a thirty-day silent Ignatian retreat.

Others, however, could not or did not want to retreat all by themselves, and this, too, is an important part of our story. Over the five years of the project, it became increasingly evident that differences in gender and in family contexts shape the meaning and locus of sabbatical. Pastors who are also primary caregivers of children or elderly parents simply could not remove themselves from their ordinary contexts in the way that we had imagined a sabbatical would entail. Thus, while the program encouraged pastors to remove themselves from their congregations, to travel and to get fresh perspective, for some of our pastors the very ordinary context of the home was the locus of their sabbatical experience. These pastors were perhaps like the apostles a bit further along in the Markan story, surrounded by the great, hungry crowd, hearing Jesus' less famous call: "You give them something to eat" (Mark 6:37).

Can there be Sabbath in the midst of the great crowd—or in the small community of the family? For some who stayed close to home, sabbatical was not restful as they maintained or assumed more domestic duties. A father who was primary caregiver of his school-aged children found himself continuing with ordinary routines and responsibilities—taking children to school, bringing them to activities—and sometimes yearning for more of the freedom that other pastors on sabbatical described. Sometimes sabbatical produced a subtle shifting in the domestic division of labor. Being at home more provided a new perspective for some male pastors who came away with greater appreciation for the work their wives did at home. Craig

French of Syracuse reflected that his sabbatical "contributed, however, to my *finally* (my wife would love hearing this) listening to her say, 'Uh, you know you really should spend more time at home.' And so I am doing more of that now—trying to be more balanced with my life. . . . I am changing some of my behaviors at home in terms of the amount of time and my commitment there." Wes Phillips of El Paso said that while solitude was appealing to him, he didn't feel that would be fair to his wife. Being at home more during sabbatical gave him "new insight" into his wife's workload; he now does dishes and laundry and feels it is a joy to share more in the work at home. He adds that he finds his quiet time in the bathroom.

The home was a welcome locus of sabbatical for some pastors who are mothers of young children. For Anna Olson of Los Angeles, sabbatical came during an exhausting second trimester of pregnancy and, after she gave up her "to do" list, it became a receptive time for physical rest, nurture of her body, listening, and "reconnecting with family and the gift of family in my life." Sandie Richards, mother of elementary school children and also from Los Angeles, said that "the Thomas Merton experience is not available to me right now and even if it were I would not want it." Rather, she found that being able to attend to domestic things, improving her space, and creating intentional times for family was "restful for me."

We might see these different sabbatical contexts—the place apart, on the one hand, and the more familiar context of the home, on the other hand—in terms of complementary traditions of spirituality. One is desert spirituality and the practice of retreat and pilgrimage—physical journeys out of the comfortable to reflect and stimulate a spiritual transformation. The early desert fathers and mothers left cities and towns in the third, fourth, and fifth centuries to face demons and cultivate purity of heart in the deserts of Egypt, Palestine, and Syria. Douglas Burton-Christie described this desert spirituality: "They lived their lives within a kind of rhythm of withdrawal, encounter, and return."[7] The other tradition is more rooted, less about withdrawal and return and more about staying and creating sacred space in the ordinary. Here the Jewish practice of Shabbat may guide—centered in and sanctifying the home, marked by ordinary domestic rituals like cleaning, cooking, lighting candles, eating, and drinking. Shabbat serves as a protected time during the week for family within the larger Jewish community. It is a time for rest, prayer, play, feasting, study, and celebration. The ongoing practice of Sabbath keeping in Judaism, a family-centered faith, could inform Christian pastors seeking to balance the needs of their congregation with time apart for self and family. It also could be quite helpful for laypeople, who rarely have the luxury of an extended eight-week period away from home, as they seek to grow into Sabbath practices.

SABBATICAL AND FAMILY

In fact, as pastors spent more time at home and pulled back from the demands of urban ministry, some saw the toll that ministry had taken on their family lives. Sabbatical became an opportunity for repentance, reconciliation, and restoration within the family. One pastor realized that he had neglected his teenage children, and he made a serious commitment to repairing the relationships. Another pastor said that the sabbatical literally saved her marriage and helped her to clarify her multiple vocations and commitments. She realized that she needed to create more boundaries around her time with family. A congregation can get another pastor, she came to believe, but the children have only one mother.

Some pastors intentionally followed a model of Shabbat as family—rather than individual—practice. Lewis Nicholson and his wife Cynthia carved out every Friday as their own Sabbath time and noted: "We just have that sabbatical mode in our family life that really makes our life a whole lot better and a whole lot more balanced." Trish McRae of San Diego said that her family takes Sunday as a Sabbath day together:

Keeping the Sabbath holy—when I realized that I need to do this, it changed our whole family life. No homework, no housework, no laundry on Sundays—that especially goes for me—it is our time together as a family after church. I have no evening service, and sometimes when we have a church activity, like going to a movie, our family will go together as well. But that has really stuck—it's crucial for the pastor's kids, crucial for my marriage, crucial for me. I need that, I need that.

Of course, it was not always easy to create family Sabbath time. Meshing schedules for all family members can be challenging. Some female pastors noted that with children in school all week and church on Sunday, the few free moments of weekend time are the only window for catching up on shopping, cleaning, cooking, and other errands with the family. Others observed that while sabbatical for male pastors might mean reconnecting with spouse or children with whom they had lost touch, for women pastors who were on call constantly at church and at home, true sabbatical rest had to mean some relief also from domestic duties.

And while many pastors struggled to juggle the demands of ministry and family, single pastors also faced challenges in creating boundaries. Debra Collins of El Paso remarked: "Since I am single, I often make myself too available and do not get away from the ministry as much as I should. This [the sabbatical] provided me the physical rest I needed. It also showed me how important it is to be intentional in getting away and resting."

PREPARATION FOR SABBATICAL

We have learned that in order to maximize the value of sabbatical, it is critical that pastors receive support and guidance in preparing for their leave. The orientation retreat at Boston University offered pastors theological frameworks and practical guidelines for sabbatical so that they could begin their leave time with reflection and intentionality. Sabbath, of course, was our major theme, and we invited pastors to consider what Sabbath practices they might cultivate in their own contexts. We talked with pastors about how to clearly delegate responsibilities prior to going on leave and how to negotiate boundaries with congregation members and staff. We noted that even informal contact with staff or members quickly degenerates into responsibility (unlike other professions, a pastor is frequently considered "on the job" even during informal conversation with parishioners). We suggested that pastors consider coming to the church only at odd hours to pick up important mail or materials. Together we considered what would constitute a crisis or emergency about which the pastor should be contacted; for example, a funeral might, but a baptism would likely not as it probably could be rescheduled.

Perhaps more important was the opportunity for participants to hear from fellow pastors who were just completing their sabbatical leaves. Their colleagues described the power of sabbatical in their own lives and ministries. They also shared what they had learned about what to do and what not to do. They offered ideas about how to prepare congregations for the pastor's sabbatical and, even better, how to invite them to develop Sabbath practices alongside the pastor. They encouraged one another to take time to rest and care for self and family. To a person, pastors recommended taking the maximum time available, as it takes time to ease into Sabbath mode. Pastors' own honest stories of sabbatical are important testimonies and should be shared with peers and denominational leaders.

A number of pastors noted the intensive work it takes to prepare to go out on sabbatical. Many felt that they had to complete everything in the office, even working ahead several months, in order to leave their congregations. Thus, for some, the preparation for sabbatical was exhausting. This is a difficult tension, perhaps also reflected in the work of Jewish women who clean, shop, and cook to prepare the house for Shabbat. In his book *The Sabbath*, Abraham Joshua Heschel counsels: "Rest on the Sabbath as if all your work were done."[8]

This advice to accept the incompleteness of our work may be difficult to enact.

Lorraine Anderson of Boston reflected on her preparation for sabbatical, which included sage counsel from spiritual directors and a gradual sinking into rest:

> In preparation for my leave time, I prayed much and consulted with two spiritual directors, who offered very practical suggestions. For example, one said, "Just because you have the time to do something doesn't mean you should do it. Let everything you do come out of a place of rest." The other suggested months earlier that I begin asking God for one or two "Sabbath-type gifts" right away, rather than bottling it all up until the leave time began. I decided to pray that God would "massage my soul and massage my body."

Anderson's practice of Sabbath keeping and her attempt to midwife Sabbath to those in trauma in Boston brought her to new language for God: she called the God she was discovering "the Great Masseur."

RETURN FROM SABBATICAL

How do urban pastors sustain their new insights and ways of being once their sabbatical is over? Does the experience of a paid leave change them or their congregations in any sustained way? Many pastors indicate that they have retained some form of Sabbath practice, whether a regular day off, weekly family time, or a yearly retreat. Dan Haas, of Aurora, Illinois, takes Monday off now; he noted that "having the 'permission to do so' the first time was very helpful." The experience of sabbatical also shapes *how* pastors take time off—with more intentionality, less as a day for errands, more focus on reflection and self-nurture. Many pastors try very hard to protect some regular time off for life-giving, life-affirming space and activities. Some continue practices that they cultivated during their sabbatical, such as prayer, journaling, study, art, and exercise. Some suggest that while they have not been able to sustain such practices in the course of their ongoing ministry, the memory of the practices (or their tangible sabbatical creations) serves as a kind of reminder to them of a fullness that is possible, that they have experienced. One pastor said that sabbatical serves as a kind of radar for when she needs to stop, pull back, rest. Joan Murray of Boston similarly said that while sustaining Sabbath practices was difficult upon her return to ministry, "what is different for me now than at any other time I can remember is that I have a touchstone—I know what it is like to feel rested and to take care of myself. I know what Sabbath feels like and I know the telltale signs when I begin to lose balance in my life."

The lasting effects need more study. Many pastors noted a rise in their energy, greater balance, and clarity in their sense of vocation immediately upon returning from sabbatical. They wanted very much to continue to live out of their sabbatical transformation. Upon her return to ministry following her time in Alaska, Claudia Rowe reflected: "The transformative power of the experiencing of this goodness of God, in which I have believed, will be ongoing. I long to respond to people out of that endless generosity, rather than out of the sense of straightened resources that stress often produces in my psyche."

Others expressed less optimism about the possibility of sustaining Sabbath rhythms in ongoing ministry. When asked whether the sabbatical caused him to develop any Sabbath practices that have continued, one pastor responded: "It caused a Sabbath ache. I can't say that it altered my workaholism very much." Elaine Peresluha of Bangor called the pastoral enrichment leave "a tease." "Five weeks was just long enough to give me a taste of what distance and time away from the office, the calls and demands of ministry, can do for one's spirit. I need more." The leave was a helpful beginning in that: "I have not perfected the structure of my boundaries yet, but at least I have a few of the fence posts up so I know where they need to be erected." Writing about the beautiful openness and grace of her sabbatical experiences, one pastor reflected: "The scary part, for me, has been the inability to sustain that."

Pastors' ability to sustain Sabbath practices depends in part on how congregations experience and respond to the sabbatical and the pastor's reentry, and how the congregation's culture, leadership, and spirituality change as a result. Congregations at times were suspicious or resentful of their pastor's sabbatical. Some suspected that the pastor was looking for another job and would be leaving the church. Others did not understand the concept of sabbatical or resented their pastor taking one because, after all, most laypersons do not have the opportunity to take a sabbatical from work. At times the dynamics in a congregation already were difficult or dysfunctional and the pastor faced heightened opposition upon returning from sabbatical.

Still, pastors' sabbaticals clearly can benefit congregations as the pastor returns with a larger vision for the church or revived energy for ministry. Craig French pointed to Sabbath as a practice of play and delight: "Learning to relax will help me find ways to bring that exuberance and playfulness into the life of the parish and its ministries." Kurt Christenson, a Lutheran pastor in Springfield, Massachusetts, used the time to conceive of a new governing structure for his church: "We got rid of the whole church council and completely restructured when I came back." Sandie Richards described the sabbatical as a "'reset' button in that we were able to recalibrate the dynamics of our church."

Pastors' leave also can empower lay leadership in a congregation. Frances Howell, pastor of Miller Inner City United Methodist Church in Savannah, Georgia, commented: "I can tell you without reservation that it affected the leadership of the congregation because they feel more of the responsibilities now. Before, they didn't, they felt the ministries were totally the pastor's responsibility. . . . I didn't know how to let go. I felt that I needed to be there in order for things to move, to go on. After the sabbatical, I started seeing that if I manage ministry properly, by empowering my leaders and delegating responsibilities, the church could go on without me. What is happening now is that I am able to take off to attend training events, participate in other programs, and do other things, and the church continues to move on."

Clearly, pastors are better able to sustain Sabbath practices when congregations are invited into those practices. Roman Catholic priest Joseph Muth started doing regular sabbatical days off with his entire parish staff and invited staff from several parishes across the diocese of Baltimore to join together in a day of prayer and retreat. After his return from pastoral leave, Lewis Nicholson preached a series of messages on the importance of the Sabbath as a biblical paradigm and spiritual practice for Christian believers. The month of July 2005 was declared as "Church at Rest" where the church only assembled for Sunday morning worship. Members were encouraged to rest, read, and reflect, a practice they have maintained. Nicholson notes: "As a matter of fact, I have been able to diminish my operational ministerial functions because I have left in place those leaders who assumed my duties while away. This has freed me to give myself more to reading and studying the Word of God, making me more effective as a pastor, preacher, and teacher."

Sabbatical is very important for pastors and potentially empowering for congregations. However, it is unrealistic to expect that pastors can sustain Sabbath practices in a vacuum. They need congregational ecologies that support these practices, beginning not just for the seasoned pastor but also for lay staff and student interns. And while sabbatical may not be available for most laity, laypersons still can be invited and formed into Sabbath practices appropriate to their own contexts. Sabbath practices should not be rationalized simply on instrumental grounds (e.g., we'll give sabbatical to the pastor so that she can work more effectively for us) but rather as core to the identity and worship of the whole congregation.

SABBATH PRACTICES AND PASTORAL EXCELLENCE

Unfortunately, pastors and congregations too often describe sabbatical in instrumental terms—as a way to increase their productivity, efficiency, or effectiveness. And this is understandable, as some pastors have an uphill battle in securing a sabbatical from their congregations. Even well-intentioned congregations may be puzzled about the purpose of a sabbatical. Moreover, all are part of a larger culture that prizes doing more, faster. Perhaps this is why one pastor prefaced his sermon about his upcoming sabbatical with this version of an oft-quoted story about two lumberjacks having a log cutting competition:

> One of the lumberjacks worked feverishly throughout the contest, swinging his axe without rest to the point of exhaustion. The other lumberjack worked at a more leisurely pace. Even in the midst of the competition he took several breaks while his competitor was chopping away. When the contest ended, much to everyone's surprise, the second lumberjack had cut the most logs and was declared the winner. The first lumberjack was furious, "How could you win? How could you have cut more logs than me? Why, you even stopped to take some breaks in the midst of the cutting!" The second lumberjack replied, "Yes indeed, I took a few breaks. But what you failed to notice was that during my breaks I was sharpening my axe."[9]

And yet, Sabbath is not really about sharpening one's axe. Heschel writes: "To the biblical mind . . . the Sabbath as a day of rest, as a day of abstaining from toil, is not for the purpose of recovering one's lost strength and becoming fit for the forthcoming labor. The Sabbath is a day for the sake of life."[10] Another Jewish theologian, Aryeh Kaplan, describes Sabbath rest as a time for "relinquishing our mastery over the world." In this, we emulate God, who rested on the seventh day not because God was tired but as a way of no longer "asserting . . . mastery over the universe."[11]

Sabbath keeping can make pastors more excellent, not in an instrumental sense of recharging their batteries for more work, but in a deeper sense. Sabbath keeping is a practice that embodies and cultivates the very virtues and habits that constitute pastoral excellence—and those include a kind of awe and wonder of God, a sense of freedom, delight, prayerfulness, humility, and receptivity to God's grace. Lewis Nicholson used the metaphor of "emptiness" to describe the call of Sabbath: "All musical instruments make music when they are empty, e.g., drums; it is possible that God can breathe through us and make music through us." Quaker pastor Steve Pedigo also noted the receptive character of Sabbath rest, which "isn't something I can do [but] something I have to receive." Curtis Edmunds spoke of allowing himself "to be poured into." Far from being the strategy of a clever woodcutter, Sabbath practices entail and develop habits of receiving, listening, pausing, praising, and delighting.

Practices are carried by communities over time; they are links to those who have gone before us in faith. Practices not only reflect or apply what we believe; they actually help us to understand, to grasp knowledge of ourselves and God. We grow in wisdom through what we do. Craig Dykstra argues that through participation in practices "we may come to awareness of certain realities that outside of these practices are beyond our ken."[12] Practices then witness to our beliefs about God and ourselves; simultaneously they form us, bringing us to know God and our own vocations more closely. The practice of Sabbath keeping yields an embodied knowledge, as Dorothy C. Bass notes: "Keeping Sabbath, Christian practitioners come to know in their bones that creation is God's gift, that God does not intend that anyone should work without respite."[13] Sabbath practices embody and reveal knowledge of God as Creator and Liberator, then, inviting us to imitate that divine rhythm of work and rest. Sabbath practices are not just helpful in sustaining pastors; we would argue that they are an integral dimension of pastoral excellence itself.

4

Renewing the Spirit

Create in me a clean heart, O God, and put a new and right
spirit within me.

(Ps. 51:10)

Trish McRae has served Chollas View United Methodist
Church, a small congregation in southeast San Diego, for fifteen years. McRae is an energetic pastor but she realizes more
and more that she cannot do the work on her own fuel alone:

It's impossible to face the violence, the poverty, the despair
that is a daily occurrence in my urban setting on my own
strength and wisdom. My peace of mind is dependent on
guidance from God, and my congregation needs its shepherd to be dependent on God because being spiritually
aware and keen to all of what we must face as a community is often a life or death matter. The battles we face in
my urban community come as suddenly as a rash of gang
shootings or as subtly as the political maneuverings of the
school board trying to close all of our high schools. The
importance of prayer has been brought home to me in a
revitalized way.

McRae is not alone in seeing a deep spiritual life as critical
to urban ministry, nor is she alone in struggling sometimes to
sustain spiritual disciplines amid her work. Urban pastors

often express a hunger for a renewed spirituality and readily acknowledge that their ministry can actually squeeze out time for the very practices that they say are essential to sustaining their spirits.

Sabbath keeping is a central practice of spiritual renewal. In some ways, it is a meta-practice, as it entails and generates other practices that give life to the spirit, such as prayer, reading, reflection, silence, play, and nurture of self and others. Urban pastors' experiences point to rich possibilities for connecting pastors to traditions of Christian and Jewish spirituality, which offer wisdom and guidance for cultivating such practices. While disciplines such as prayer and silence are grounding to ministry in any context, they offer important alternative experiences of time and relationship in the urban context. It is clear, too, that the spirituality at the heart of urban pastoral excellence will encompass nurture of the body, joyful play, and other forms of self-care.

A PRAYER FOR RENEWAL

Psalm 51 offers a prayer for renewal that is rooted in a deep sense of human dependence on God's grace. The psalmist acknowledges to God the depth of his sin and pleads for cleansing and new life: "Create in me a clean heart, O God, and put a new and right spirit within me" (Ps. 51:10). The spiritual renewal of the person depends on God's mercy and grace—the human spirit needing infusion of God's own breath or spirit. The renewal of the human spirit is a work of God's creation, just as in Genesis God breathes life into the first human (Gen. 2:7). Thus, the psalmist begs: "Do not cast me away from your presence, and do not take your holy spirit from me" (Ps. 51:11). For it is God's spirit that sustains his own: "Restore to me the joy of salvation, and sustain in me a willing spirit" (Ps. 51:12).

Spiritual renewal is not a project or program but rather an ongoing dynamic in the relationship between God and persons. It could be described as a kind of re-creation. Ultimately, spiritual renewal is a work of God's mercy and grace, aided by human intentionality, prayer, confession, and hope in God's power to transform. In seeking to serve as ministers of God's grace in the city, urban pastors like all persons need continual renewal. In fact, we cannot talk of sustaining pastoral excellence without talking about pastors' ongoing spiritual renewal, for receptivity to God's spirit precedes any work of ministry. If only God's spirit would re-create his own, says the psalmist, *then* he would teach transgressors God's ways, bring sinners back, declare God's praises, and proclaim God's power to deliver (Ps. 51:13–15).

CHALLENGES OF SPIRITUAL DISCIPLINES

In the Sustaining Urban Pastoral Excellence program, urban pastors were asked to be attentive to their spiritual lives and to engage in practices that would foster spiritual renewal. Many pastors affirmed the importance of spiritual disciplines for grounding and sustaining pastoral excellence in the city. Dan Haas of Aurora, Illinois, wrote: "If your . . . soul and spirit is not growing and at peace with God, the sheer intensity of urban problems will overwhelm and crush you." They also shared with us the difficulties of maintaining those disciplines amid the demands of urban ministry. Wes Philips of El Paso noted: "A tenacious pursuit of personal spiritual discipline is one of the most important practices—in the urban context there are so many additional voices competing for time and energy."

As pastors noted, attempts at renewal too often are prompted by crisis. Particularly in the urban context, where pastors move from one crisis to another with little time for reflection or self-care, a more intentional, structured integration is needed. As Walter Mueller of El Paso put it: "It is too easy to drift through life and disregard continuous personal growth and renewal. The moment of crisis is not the time to lay spiritual foundations. You cope with crisis with whatever spiritual, emotional, intellectual, and physical resources you have built into your life up to that moment."

TURNING THE VOLUME DOWN:
CULTIVATING SILENCE

Clearly, companionship helps greatly as one builds those spiritual foundations; in fact, community is integral to the Christian life. As discussed in chapter 2, holy friendships not only
offer peer support, prayer, accountability, and safe space, but
the practice of friendship itself is a dimension of pastoral excellence. Pastors greatly value friendships. They also note the
importance of wise mentors, counselors, and spiritual directors.
Some work hard to develop ecumenical and civic partnerships
to address the needs of their communities. Many point to the
gift of family. Certainly, urban pastors identify the cultivation
of community as terribly important in nurturing their spirits.

As important as these relationships are, the intentional cultivation of silence and solitude also can be life giving to the
urban pastor. Steve Goodier, of Salt Lake City, wrote: "Balanc-
ing the demands upon my life and living it out in a busy and
complex environment challenges my ability to remain serene,
at best, and sane, at worst. Furthermore, quiet reflection and
alone time are too often missing in urban ministry. Where do
you go to get away from it all? I need to regularly find the times
and places to 'let my soul catch up with my body.'"

Silence is highly valued in many traditions of Christian spirituality, though often elusive in the city. Pastors nonetheless
drew inspiration from Scriptures and monastic traditions as
they sought out pockets of silence in the urban context. Some
studied the Desert Fathers and Mothers, those early monastics
who understood silence as an essential discipline. The silence
the *abbas* and *ammas* practiced in the desert was not a comfortable respite but rather part of spiritual warfare—a stark means
of confronting their own sinfulness, battling demons, and seeking true wisdom and peace. Abbot Pastor said: "Any trial whatever that comes to you can be conquered by silence." Another
saying recounts that Abbot Agatho carried a stone in his mouth
for three years "until he learned to keep silent." Silence was
understood as important in avoiding vices and keeping focus on

God: "One of the elders said: A monk ought not to inquire how this one acts, or how that one lives. Questions like this take us away from prayer and draw us on to backbiting and chatter. There is nothing better than to keep silent." While many sought a "word of life" from the desert *abbas* and *ammas*, the monastics believed that silence itself can teach more than words. When the Bishop of Alexandria journeyed to Scete, the monks asked Abbot Pambo to give the bishop a word. The abbot replied: "If he is not edified by my silence, there is not hope that he will be edified by my words."[1]

It is a great distance from the Egyptian desert of Scete to contemporary New York City. Still, Frank Barker, who pastors a small Moravian church in the Little India section of Lower Manhattan, looks to the Desert Fathers and Mothers as spiritual guides. Though far from a monastic setting (a nearby Indian restaurant emits its curry flavor into the church sanctuary from time to time), Barker finds the early desert traditions of Christian spirituality grounding and relevant to his own spirituality and ministry. In particular, he values the practice of silence and seeks to teach his congregation how to be silent in the midst of the noise of Manhattan.

The value placed on silence in the early desert tradition is apparent too in the sixth-century *Rule of Saint Benedict*, which became the guiding rule for monastic communities for centuries. Several of our Protestant urban pastors indicated that they are informed by Benedictine spirituality. Pastor Barker, for example, draws from the Benedictine rule guidance on maintaining a spirit of silence. He spent part of his sabbatical traveling to Nicaragua to learn more about the culture of his parishioners. His one regret, he noted, was that he used the Internet while away and thus kept contact with New York. It was, by his understanding of Benedictine spirituality, an interruption of his silence. Barker points to Benedict's discussion of the importance of silence in the monastery, in which Benedict (drawing from Psalm 39, Proverbs 10:19, and Proverbs 18:21) advises monks that the disciples' part is to be silent and to listen.[2]

Amid the din of the city, urban pastors simply need to "turn the volume all the way down and fall in love with the silence of rejuvenation," as Mark Smith of Aurora, Illinois, said. Silence can be a spiritual "well"—a way of drawing living water. It is not always comfortable; for some it may be oppressive. Some grow into the practice. One pastor found it very difficult to be silent during his sabbatical, but he now practices silence regularly. He follows the rule of Benedict and attends a local vespers service whenever he can. Before this, he said, he was "addicted to busy." Silence represents a dedication to God that helps him to distinguish between the "urgent" and the "important." Another pastor engages in silent meditation twice daily and practices listening, particularly with his wife: "Don't criticize, comment, or offer advice. Offer her the gift of listening and being heard."

Urban pastors are constantly with people, and often the only way to find silence is to carve out moments of solitude. Marlene and Steve Pedigo are Quakers who together led the Chicago Fellowship of Friends ministry, a multicultural congregation situated in the middle of the Cabrini-Green public housing development on the north side of Chicago. Now demolished amid gentrification of the neighborhood, Cabrini-Green was a massive series of high-rise and row buildings housing a largely African American population. Residents suffered high unemployment and school dropout rates, and the neighborhood was plagued by violent gang turf wars. The Pedigos sought to embody the peacemaking that is central to the Quaker witness in this inner-city Chicago context. Marlene relied on spiritual disciplines—including the practices of silence, listening, and worship that are integral to the Quaker tradition—to sustain her in ministry. She wrote: "The practices which sustain me in urban ministry have been prayer, solitude, Scripture reading, and corporate worship. In urban ministry it is easy to find your life 'full' of people, stressful schedules, and crisis. The spiritual disciplines allowed me to 'empty' the stress of urban ministry out of my life, to reflect and pray about circumstances, to reflect upon Scripture, and to listen to God for answers."

The Quaker tradition places a great value on silence, understood as deep stillness and listening for the voice of the Spirit. Silence is not necessarily a solitary practice, as the community worships together in silence as well. As the nineteenth-century British Friend Caroline Stephens wrote:

> The silence we value is not the mere outward silence of the lips. It is a deep quietness of heart and mind, a laying aside of all preoccupation with passing things—yes, even with the workings of our own minds. . . . This "silence of all flesh" appears to us to be the essential preparation for any act of true worship. It is also, we believe, the essential condition at all times of inward illumination. . . . It is the experience, I believe, of all those who have been most deeply conscious of his revelations of himself, that they are made emphatically to the "waiting" soul—to the spirit which is most fully conscious of its own inability to do more than wait in silence before him."[3]

God's voice can be heard amid crowds and noise. As the contemplative Taizé religious community notes, God spoke to Moses and the Israelites at Sinai in a great clamor of thunder and trumpets (Exod. 19:16–19).[4] And yet, when we become so accustomed to noise, God may wait for silence before speaking, as happened with the prophet Elijah. Elijah, a "zealous" servant of the Lord, waited for Yahweh to speak to him. A great wind passed by, but the Lord was not in the wind, nor in an earthquake, nor in fire. After the fire, there was "a sound of sheer silence," and only then did Elijah go out to hear God's voice: "What have you been doing here, Elijah" (1 Kgs. 19:11–13). It is a question that could be posed again and again—asking for an accounting, for discernment. In the text, Elijah responds to the Lord, who then gives him direction about what he is to do next.

Chauncey Brown of Syracuse, New York, described his time alone with God as a kind of Elijah experience. Free of the need to "be all things to all people," which he felt regularly in his pastoral duties, he was able to "just talk to God for me" and "to listen to me." Practices such as Bible reading took on a different meaning: "I could read my Bible not for a sermon but for a sermon to me." In a vocation that could involve constant interaction, practices of silence and solitude create space, realign relationships, and remind pastors of the primary relationship that grounds all others.

MARKING TIME: THE RHYTHM OF PRAYER

If silence and solitude realign relationships, prayer may have the capacity to restructure time. Urban pastors repeatedly note the rapid pace of life in the city; as Dan Haas said: "The pace of city life is warp speed and it does not let up." The lightning speed of life impacts spirituality and ministry and even shapes people's sense of time. Sabbath practices offer a corrective to a warped sense of time, inviting us into divine rhythms of work and rest instead of the 24–7 mentality. Prayer, too, serves as an important centering practice that offers a slower and more natural sense of time. David Hughes of Springfield, Massachusetts, reflected that discipline of daily times of devotion is "a crucially important centering experience. . . . This discipline is especially helpful in an urban setting, where the pace of life is so quick that it can be very easy to lose contact with our spiritual source of strength in God." In describing the importance of spiritual disciplines, Altagracia Perez of Los Angeles wrote: "I think that these disciplines are essential for everyone. The difference in the urban context is the pace and the complexity. If time is not taken, if the breath and thought are not slowed down, the pace runs the work instead of a thoughtful, prayerful plan."

It may seem like common sense to say that pastors need to pray. In his letter to the Thessalonians, the apostle Paul instructed the Christian community to "rejoice always, pray without ceasing, and give thanks in all circumstances, for this is the will of God in Christ Jesus for you" (1 Thess. 5:16–18). Whatever else it is, the church is a community of prayer. The pastor of the church must be a person of prayer who can gather a community of prayer.

Even well-intentioned ministers, however, can move away from the practices that are at the heart of excellent ministry. Urban pastors indicate a great desire to deepen their prayer lives. They repeatedly note that prayer is crucial to their ministry but acknowledge that they sometimes do not pray as regularly or do not enjoy prayer as much as they hope to. Supported by peers and given sabbatical time to recenter, pastors often discover new forms of prayer in the tradition or renew their commitment to existing habits of prayer.

One pastor set aside early morning time daily, noting that the scriptural text Mark 1:35 had taken on a whole new context in his life. The text reads: "In the morning, while it was still very dark, [Jesus] got up and went out to a deserted place, and there he prayed." Reading further, we see that Jesus' disciples find him in his quiet moment and tell him, "Everyone is searching for you." And with that, Jesus leaves the solitude to go to neighboring towns and proclaim the message there (vv. 36–39). Perhaps the passage embodies the tensions or rhythms of urban ministry—carving out almost stolen moments of solitude and prayer before giving oneself over to the crowds and the ministry for which one came.

Some pastors gravitated to the traditional monastic practice of the "divine office" (literally, the service of God), also called the "liturgy of the hours." The office structures the day around regular times of prayer, from morning through night, centered largely on the chanting of the psalms. This pattern enacts Psalm 119:164: "Seven times a day I praise you for your righteous ordinances." In the Benedictine tradition, the office or *opus dei* ("work of God") sets the rhythm of the day and serves as the bond of the community. According to the *Rule*: "At the hour for the Divine Office, as soon as the signal is heard, let them abandon whatever they may have in hand and hasten with the greatest speed, yet with seriousness, so that there is no excuse for levity. Let nothing, therefore, be put before the Work of God."[5] In monasteries today, sounds of bells still call the community to prayer, and all work at hand is put aside for prayer. Jennifer Gutierrez, who directs the Office of Urban Ministry for the United Methodist California-Pacific conference, wrote that the practice of praying the office "helps me to reconnect with God in time, especially in an urban context that so deeply values the shaping and reshaping of space, and is very disconnected from the natural rhythms of the earth."

Kurt Christenson of Springfield found that the sabbatical gave him permission to be still, which led to more time in prayer. He then sought to sustain that prayer in his ongoing ministry, not out of a sense of obligation but because he sees it sustaining his ministry: "Returning to active parish life has intensified my desire to reorder my days around prayer. It has been this activity which has most altered my daily urban ministry activity—giving it renewed power and clarity." Wenton Fyne of New York City commented: "The city moves at a different pace. A systematic prayer life builds inner strength and provides stability and balance in my own spiritual journey."

That stability and balance is indispensable as pastors confront great suffering. Joan Murray, who served as pastor of the outdoor Common Cathedral church in Boston, continues to practice many of the Ignatian prayers and practices that she learned on her thirty-day sabbatical retreat. She also values periodic time apart, spiritual companionship and direction, Eucharist, and time to do nothing. She writes:

> I am not sure any of this is different for urban ministers than it is for ministers in other settings. However, I do know that my ministry is very intense and that I feel "out there"—literally outside and outside the box (no building, church outside, street ministry), often in view of my parishioners as I minister to others of them, and I often feel very vulnerable . . . the trauma of their lives [which] challenges me—mental illness, addiction, mental retardation, chronic physical illness, sleeping in shelters and on the street (I am not sure which is worse—many claim the shelters are less safe), and more. I would say that all the practices I have mentioned

are even more important when one is ministering to people in great need, especially because it is so easy to absorb the trauma of their lives, to be overly invested in trying to solve their problems, and to be easily manipulated.

Prayer often leads to self-examination and discernment, practices that take time and courage, a willingness to be vulnerable in the safety of God's presence, and a willingness to change. Psalm 139 reads: "Search me, O God, and know my heart; test me and know my thoughts. See if there is any wicked way in me, and lead me in the way everlasting" (vv. 23–24). With some time and space for reflection, pastors entered into this kind of prayerful vulnerability. For some it led to uncomfortable realizations about the state of their relationships, faith, or vocation. Several pastors saw that they needed help in setting boundaries (they described this as a "growing edge"). Trish McRae commented that she needed to undertake "deliberate examination of my schedule . . . what was important versus what was urgent, masquerading as important." One pastor said that the unhurried time he gave to Bible reading and prayer led to some disturbing introspection: "I found myself faced with a growing dissatisfaction with my life on virtually every front: family, financial, professional, etc. I didn't like what I saw in myself. I realized that I had become what Solomon described as a 'backslider in heart' in Proverbs 14:14a." The pastor took a retreat and was able to "review all that the Lord had revealed to me," eventually coming to a sense that "Christ was more fully formed in me as a result." A number of pastors found that with prayer and Sabbath rest they came to clarity about some aspect of their vocations. Shortly before embarking on her sabbatical, Episcopal priest Anna Olson of Los Angeles left her parish and began a leadership position in an organization fighting for workers' rights. Her sabbatical enabled her to prayerfully explore questions about her path—how to carve out new ways of being a priest within a hierarchical structure, how to balance ministry and family, how to live the life that God is calling her to live.

NOT BY BREAD ALONE: LIVING BY THE WORD

Christian prayer goes hand in hand with immersion in the Scriptures. From the earliest traditions of Christian spirituality, prayer was scripturally based, as described above in the practice of the daily office. Scriptural prayer also is the norm in the ancient practice of *lectio divina*, or holy reading, which involves a slow, meditative reading of Scripture. Urban pastors, too, emphasize the importance of prayerful Bible study. Wenton Fyne wrote: "There must be intentional time for Bible study and reflection. One can get so busy with the energy of the city and the pressure of the pastoral work that Bible study time becomes difficult. Excellence in practice means being knowledgeable in the word."

Urban pastors express a love of the Bible and lean on it in their ministry. Ronnie Joyner of Hampton Roads, Virginia, wrote: "The Word of God is the substance of the delight. It serves as the primary ingredient in obtaining the mind of God upon my context in ministry." Tamie Allen of El Paso described her practice in terms of spiritual warfare: "Another practice I found to be helpful was praying the Scriptures, reading the word aloud and claiming God's deliverance and victory over the spiritual warfare I was encountering. Dealing with the urban context in which I minister, I have learned to depend on prayer and God's strength for understanding and clarity to minister more effectively."

Claudia Rowe of Seattle cited "the discipline of the Word" as a key practice in sustaining pastoral excellence. She does not see this discipline as more necessary for urban pastors than for any other pastor, but rather: "Every minister must reinterpret the Word in his/her own context and for his/her own people in every generation." In Rowe's view, preparing for preaching "is the greatest discipline in Bible meditation in Christendom." She also has found *lectio divina* to be a very fruitful practice in the past ten years.

Lewis Nicholson described his love of *lectio divina* this way: "It is like eating natural food for nourishment. The food, in time, as it is processed, becomes part of us. The scripture calls it *The Bread of Life.* Jesus says, '*A man should not live by bread alone but by every word that proceeds out the mouth of God*' (Matthew 4:4). So, it becomes a life which is nourished, strengthened and renewed each day by the Word of God over which one has prayed and contemplated."[6]

READING AND REFLECTION

When we began this work, we saw "study" as one of the central practices of urban pastoral excellence. Teams of pastors had to designate a study question when they applied to participate, and that question became a focal point of their bi-weekly meetings. Pastors appreciated having a focus, particularly as they got to know one another and developed a level of trust. The study question gave them structure and initial purpose. What we had not anticipated was that many pastors would come to experience a conflict between the charge to study together and the charge to cultivate Sabbath practices. Some said this was a dual message: work and be still, take on a big project and relax. In the evolving dynamic of their growth together, a number of partnerships let the "study" go. While their question still was important, what took on more life was their developing friendship and spiritual growth. Those partnerships for whom study remained important often had chosen a study question that was organic to their spiritual renewal—as in the El Paso team that asked how to sustain spiritual practice in a context isolated by the desert, or the Los Angeles group that explored models of spiritual leadership. To be sure, some teams worked quite hard, even sending out surveys and creating long bibliographies. Yet overall, what struck a chord with urban pastors was less "study" and more "reading."

Urban pastors want to read—given the chance, they dug into spiritual and theological texts; books on leadership and ministry; articles about issues in their contexts, such as immigration, divorce, and trauma; novels; and poetry. Many said that they hungered for time to read widely in the normal course of ministry. Speaking about his sabbatical, Kurt Christenson said that the time to "live in his head was glorious." Los Angeles pastor Sandie Richards found that taking time for reading was very important: "By refueling my intellect, I find I have more energy and inspiration for preaching and teaching." Wenton Fyne resolved to read one book monthly for general information.

They also cherished the space for reflection—time to think, mull over, notice, make connections, critique, imagine. The related practices of reading and reflection seemed like luxuries in the fast-paced, crisis-driven life of urban ministry. Some found that journaling was a wonderful aid to reflection. Erin Gilmore of Salt Lake City noted: "In urban ministry, most of the time we are reacting, responding in five or six different directions every day—some of it is helpful, and some of it is just because it has become habit. Writing things down helped me see and remember the things that I want to change, that I could change, to improve my ministry."

LAUGHING AND DOING WHAT YOU LOVE

Lorraine Anderson of Boston made an important discovery while on sabbatical: "There is another spiritual practice which is essential for my ministerial longevity and well-being, and that is actually doing activities that I love." As did many pastors, she came to see play not as a hobby but actually as a spiritual practice that is life-giving and life-affirming. Doing what you love need not be something reserved for a vacation or sabbatical; it was her intention and her prayer to integrate it into daily living. "I'm good at longing to do them and talking about doing them 'later on,' but not so good at actually DOING them on a regular basis! It seems so absurd! But for me, this will be a type of spiritual discipline, to go folk dancing every month; to go kayaking every couple of weeks between April and October; to walk outside every single day; to buy some snowshoes and GO snowshoeing every week in the winter; to paint rocks and make jewelry. How can I in fact do these rejuvenating things unless I schedule them into my monthly calendar? *Lord, please help me to do this."*

TAKING CARE

Time and again, urban pastors recounted stories of pastors who literally worked themselves to death. In our group discussions, they counseled one another to step out and take care of themselves, their health, and their families. They noted that competition and boasting among pastors can make self-care and acknowledgment of vulnerability more difficult. Curtis Edmonds of Hampton Roads, Virginia, learned that in order to sustain pastoral excellence, he needs to "be more open about feeling stressed and bogged down." His pastoral partnership supported him in coming to this realization: "I have been encouraged to voice it out when I feel as though the load is heavy and not look at it as a sign of weakness, but rather as an opportunity to release it so that I can be strengthened." Support for this kind of openness and self-care may be unusual among urban pastors. Edmonds's Virginia colleague Randy Fields remarked that, as an African American urban pastor, he found his experience in the Sustaining Urban Pastoral Excellence program quite out of the ordinary. In his experience, urban clergy, and particularly African American clergy, seldom plan for self-care. He came away from the program grateful for the sustained opportunity to reflect and rest and integrate the talents and gifts that God had given him for ministry.

An integrative, embodied spirituality that places a high value on wholeness and health is part of what "pastoral excellence" means. Pastors too often model a spirituality that compels them to work ceaselessly (despite biblical commands to the contrary), that does damage to their health and well-being (despite biblical descriptions of the body as the temple of the Holy Spirit), and that neglects important relationships (despite the fact that those relationships too are holy and part of their vocation). It is difficult to break out of the habits of this bound spirituality, and often congregations and fellow pastors reinforce it. Yet excellence in ministry means communicating in an embodied way—in life and not just words—the way that we are called to live by the One whose breath sustains us.

Pastors relished the sabbatical because it was generally perceived by congregations and peers to be a legitimate time apart and it gave them permission to rest and take care of themselves. Sabbath rest could become generative of practices that integrate self-care into daily living. For example, some pastors began regular exercise—from running to boxing. Others made a commitment to healthy eating. One entered intensive therapy. They described these activities as invigorating, challenging, healing, and sustaining. It also is important to name them as Christian practices. "The Christian practice of honoring the body," writes contemporary theologian Stephanie Paulsell, "is born of the confidence that our bodies are made in the image of God's own goodness. 'Your body is a temple of the Holy Spirit within you,' Paul wrote to the church at Corinth (1 Corinthians 6:19)."[7] Paulsell argues that it is possible to understand "honoring the body" as a Christian practice, despite ambiguity about the body in the Christian tradition. Such a practice "is not lying on the surface of scripture and history, like a stone in the road," she writes. "It has to be excavated, argued for, and put into dialogue with all the ways that contemporary people do and do not honor the body."[8] Urban pastors have much to contribute to that dialogue. It is only as they participate in the "argument," struggling for a model that integrates rather than disintegrates and embodies wholeness rather than self-neglect, that a more sustaining urban pastoral spirituality will emerge.

5

Finding God in the City

God is in the midst of the city; it shall not be moved;
God will help it when the morning dawns.

(Ps. 46:5).

For many Christians, the city is one of the last places to come to mind (if it comes to mind at all) when thinking about where we encounter God in our lives or find spiritual renewal. Instead our minds wander to more peaceful and serene settings outside the hurried and complex life of the city. When taking spiritual retreats, we pack our bags and head out to places where we can be more in touch with nature or find peace and quiet. We tend to be drawn, moreover, to passages of Scripture that reflect this rural serenity: "The Lord is my shepherd, I shall not want. He makes me lie down in green pastures; he leads me beside still waters" (Ps. 23:1–2). Perhaps this tendency is one reason the urban context is underrepresented in the long history of Christian spirituality, though it must also be remembered that urbanization is a relatively recent phenomenon.

There is no reason to think that pastors should be an exception to this nonurban bias when it comes to finding God; indeed, for many of the urban pastors we studied, the path to spiritual renewal and Sabbath wholeness meanders through remote mountains, sandy beaches, green forests, and national parks. The fact is that the city can be a spiritual desert for pastors. As Barbara Brown Taylor characterizes it:

> According to holy writ, there are three chief places where God reveals God's self to us: on mountaintops, in the wilderness, and in the city. The air is thin in the first; there are wild beasts in the second; but the city may be the hardest place of all to recognize the presence and activity of God. There is a lot of sin, for one thing, a lot of sadness and lostness and disorder. And there are a lot of distractions, not least of which is our busyness, our scrambling efforts to feed all the hungers we meet. It is hard to stay attentive to God's activity when we are half dead from our own.[1]

But though the city is a place of distractions, busyness, and frenzied activity and though it is often imagined in Scripture as a place of unrest, idolatry, and wickedness, it is also the holy habitation of God; as the psalmist says, "God is in the midst of the city" (46:5). One of the characteristics of ministerial excellence we have discovered among urban pastors is their awareness of and sensitivity to God's urban presence. They may leave the city from time to time to find rest and recuperation for their bodies and their spirits, but they also find ways of cultivating an attentiveness to God's presence and activity within the city. The urban context is not for them simply to be understood as the place from which we flee in order to find God "in green pastures" and "beside still waters." Rather the city can be a lively, diverse, and dynamic matrix for finding God and spiritual renewal. While the purpose of this chapter is not to argue that God can be found only or primarily in the city, it explores the way the urban context is a vibrant place of encounter with God and a site for our transformation into the people of God.

THE CITY AS SACRED PLACE

Place matters. The cities where we live, the buildings that surround us, the way land is used—all these have important effects upon us and shape our encounters with each other and with God. Throughout history, place has been of central religious importance to human beings, as attested to by the attachment of communities to particular locations; the designation of certain lands as "holy lands" or sites as shrines; the liturgical importance of objects, buildings, and places deemed sacred; and the widespread practice of pilgrimage. Yet one could argue that the significance of place has largely been lost or relegated to the margins of modern Western life. Certainly the ease of instant communication and global travel, of flying quickly over multiple places and being able to view them all from a bird's-eye perspective, has contributed to a shift in our experience from concrete place to abstract space. Electronic technology also has the effect of "displacing" us, so that our location becomes irrelevant.[2] Theologically, this shift can be traced as far back as the late medieval and Reformation interest in God's limitless power and presence that transcends any local orientation and shifts our interest to infinite space.[3] The Protestant Reformers were especially critical of any attachment of the sacred to particular places or objects, and for that reason they construed veneration of saints, relics, or other objects of pilgrimage as superstition or even idolatry. And even though Christians would affirm with the psalmist that the natural world tells "the glory of God" and "proclaims [God's] handiwork," there is a long history in Christianity of resisting the designation of particular places as *intrinsically* holy. Did not Jesus, after all, critique the association of worship with any particular place, claiming that "God is spirit, and those who worship [God] must worship in spirit and truth" (John 4:24)? For those who worship God in spirit and truth, shouldn't place be of little importance? As the author of Hebrews writes, "For here we have no lasting city, but we are looking for the city that is to come" (13:14).

In several ways, the phenomenon of urbanization, as with secularization, reinforces this characteristically modern transcendence of the particularities of place. In 1965, for example, Harvey Cox spoke glowingly in *The Secular City* about the mobility of urban life that allows humans to "reach across boundaries" and to move "from social group to social group."[4] He spoke also about the anonymity of urban life that need not be heartless just because it permits more functional, anonymous relationships (with the banker, the grocer, the insurance agent) and liberates us from provincial and traditional norms. Today, however, it could be argued that the "secular city" has failed to deliver on its promises, as rootlessness and a lack of close-knit community produce anxiety and undercut our pursuit of a common good.

In his book *The Solace of Fierce Landscapes*, which focuses on the apophatic spirituality of wilderness places, Belden Lane makes a powerful argument for the intimate connection between place and spirituality. He also laments the fact that persons living in a post-Enlightenment, technological society have difficulty perceiving that connection:

> Our concern is simply to move as quickly (and freely) as possible from one place to another. We are bereft of rituals of entry that allow us to participate fully in the places we inhabit. . . . Modern Western culture is largely shorn of attentiveness to both habitat and *habitus*. Where we live— to what we are rooted—no longer defines who we are. . . . Without a *habitus*—particularly one that is drawn, at least in part, from the rhythm of the land around us—our habitat ceases to be a living partner in the pursuit of a common wholeness. . . . Habitat turns into scenery, inconsequential background. *Habitus* is reduced to a nonsacramental, individualistic quest for transcendent experience. . . . We are, in short, a people without a "habit," with no common custom, place, or dress to lend us shared meaning.[5]

While urbanization may have contributed to this placelessness, it could also be said that cities have suffered under modern devaluations of place along with the consumerist logic that has overtaken virtually every aspect of our lives, in which function trumps place so that cities are looked upon in almost wholly instrumental terms. While cities in Europe or older cities in the United States were built with a sense of the importance of place, including public greens and commons along with distinct, vibrant, and mixed-use neighborhoods (where people eat, shop, live, work, and socialize all in one place), cities have increasingly become mere receptacles for the activities of suburbanites who retreat in the evenings to "bedroom communities" that are frequently indistinguishable from one another. Meanwhile, as Richard Rogers says, "those responsible for [cities] have tended to see it as their role to design cities to meet private material needs, rather than foster public life."[6] In the wake of this shift, downtown areas have become ghost towns, mixed-use neighborhoods a thing of the past, while shopping, working, and family life are "segregated into ghettos of single minded activity—the business park, the Housing Estate, the residential suburb—or worse still, into giant single function buildings like Shopping Centres with their own private streets (which lead nowhere) built in."[7] As Rogers concludes, "We are witnessing the destruction of the very idea of the city."[8]

A devaluation of the particularities of place has also proven well fitted for the expansion and maintenance of imperial powers throughout history. Whether Greek, Roman, Mongolian, Japanese, British, or American, imperial powers have always tried to exercise authority and control on their subjects by the imposition of a unified or totalizing order through the homogenization of place and the erasure of difference.[9] But with today's complex interrelations between nation-state, transnational political organizations (such as the United Nations or NATO), and the ambitions of a global capitalism that has thoroughly deterritorialized economics, one could argue that never before has place been more radically devalued in the service of imperial or economic values as today, thereby encouraging "a weakening of the identity of places to the point where they not only look alike but feel alike and offer the same bland possibilities for experience."[10] Again, cities have especially paid the price for this placelessness, as urban places are made to look the same as each other (or are reproduced nostalgically in Disneyland or Las Vegas), and as churches, theaters, shops, or restaurants become indistinguishable so that eating in a Hard Rock Cafe in

Rome is little different from eating at one in Denver. In the midst of this shrinking of space and a corresponding uniformity of place, is it still possible to speak of any particular place as "sacred"? Is there a sense in which, even if "we have no lasting city," we can yet experience the city as a sacred place?

If we step back for a moment from the city as sacred place to the very notion of sacred place itself, we find in the Jewish and Christian traditions both a robust emphasis on place along with a refusal to idolize place or to limit God's activity or self-revelation to any single place. In the Hebrew and Christian Scriptures, while God is the God who cannot be contained by any single place (1 Kgs. 8:27) and for whom no one can presume to build a house (2 Sam. 7), God is also the God who encounters us in and through a particular person, Christ, and in and through the particularity of places (in the burning bush, in the wilderness, at Bethel, in Jerusalem, in a cloud, on Mount Sinai, on the road to Emmaus, in the upper room). None of these places is *intrinsically* sacred, just as cities too are not in and of themselves sacred. On the contrary, places become sacred insofar as they become places of encounter with God. And because of this encounter, neither the place nor the one encountering God in that place can ever be the same. As another way of saying this, as John Inge insists, a Christian theology of place is always a relational theology, centered as it is on the three-way relationship between God, person, and place.[11] And still another way of saying this is that places such as the urban context may function sacramentally.

For the city to function sacramentally, however, means that it is neither inherently evil nor sinful. A city is a complex combination of beautiful neighborhoods, thriving shopping areas, tree-lined boulevards, sprawling university campuses, friendly parks, vacant lots, graffiti-covered overpasses, boarded-up crack houses, and abandoned cars. Yet the Christian conviction is that just such a place is capable of being hallowed by God and of becoming a place where we meet God—whether in the face of a stranger, in the laughter and play of a child, in the tears of a mother who has just been evicted, or even in the play of the sun reflecting off of a new skyscraper onto an old courthouse below. This hallowing of the city may well be reflected, as several pastors reported, in the form and content of their churches' worship, hymns, prayers, and liturgies, which have come to reflect the character of their cities, being shaped by everything from the new hopes associated with the immigrant experience to feelings of powerlessness and anonymity in the midst of depersonalizing systems.

This hallowing of urban place is not always easy nor does it come naturally, of course. As Jennifer Gutierrez, a pastor from Los Angeles, observed:

> When I was in a rural area, there was somewhat more of a natural connection to God and spirituality. There was nature all around; there was a more natural rhythm to life, more connection to the natural processes of life and the spirituality that is inherent in that. And then moving to Los Angeles, I guess now I have to be more intentional about maintaining those connections. . . . [In the city] you get your food in little packages, and you don't see a chicken walking around (well, it depends on what neighborhood you're in, actually) but you don't see cows for sure. There is a disconnect from a lot of the natural processes that sustain life. So you have to be more intentional about connecting to the sustainer. Because it's just not there like it is in the rural areas.

What Gutierrez discovered is that she was not likely to encounter the city *automatically* or *naturally* as a sacred place, but only insofar as certain practices, habits, and disciplines along with a certain timefulness embodied in Sabbath keeping opened her to that encounter. For Gutierrez, as was mentioned in chapter 4, that meant taking up the particular practice of praying the divine hours "as a way to get more in connection with: now it's morning, now it's evening, now it's mid-day" instead of the round-the-clock hustle and bustle of the city. In this way, her experiences of the city and of the people in the city were shaped by a more creation-centered and Sabbath-shaped set of rhythms that transformed her encounters with urban place, and in this way, as she reminded us, drawing upon Abraham Heschel's *Sabbath*, our experience of place is always shaped and hallowed by God "in time."

Barbara Brown Taylor suggests further practices that can aid us in finding God in the city, and this she does by drawing on the example of the Desert Mothers and Fathers already mentioned in chapters 3 and 4. Given that these desert monastics saw urban life as a "shipwreck from which they must swim or lose their lives," it may seem odd that they would have anything to teach urban-dwellers today.[12] But the Desert Mothers and Fathers did not leave the city to avoid temptation or to find safety. In the ancient world, the city was a refuge, a place with walls, a source of security and defense from attack. In contrast, the desert "was a place without walls, a place of desolation or ruin where demons roamed, a lonely place populated by jackals, vultures, ostriches, and wild asses that brayed at the moon. To live in the desert was to live undefended, to expose yourself to the elements and sleep lightly, surrounded by a whole crowd of spirits that might wish you well but more likely wished you dead."[13] But the wilderness and the city have changed places with each other or are at least more alike now, as Brown Taylor observes: "The city's walls have fallen; it is no longer a place to go to be safe but a place to go to be challenged, to wrestle the modern-day demons of corruption and excess, the beasts of homelessness and despair."[14] For pastors, as Joan Murray noted, ministry in the city means being "out there," exposed, vulnerable, engaged daily with suffering and trauma.

What is called for in pastoral ministry in the city is the "detachment, laughter, and humility" that once characterized the desert monastics. Detachment in this context is not an attitude of indifference nor is it a posture of being aloof, uninvolved, or unconcerned. It is rather "the presence of so much care that we give up our own desires and disappointments for the sake of those whom we serve."[15] It is, in other words, the surrender of our all-consuming calculations of how successful we are likely to be in our ministry and is instead a patient and humble refusal to take ourselves too seriously or to let our identities come to depend wholly on our work or on what others think of us or how they treat us. Good friends can help us in this regard—for example, to learn to laugh at ourselves, to discover the capacity to say no—so that through them we learn to "hold our lives lightly."[16] That lightness means an ability to step back periodically, to pause and rest, trusting in God and others to continue the work. It means creating space for responsiveness—rather than simple reactivity—in a place characterized by crisis.

Philip Sheldrake notes that a "spirituality of living publicly in the city has to engage with everyday life as itself a spiritual practice."[17] While traditions of Christian spirituality have emphasized the contemplative life—removed to some extent from quotidian concerns—as more perfect than the active life, Sheldrake argues for spirituality as a mode of public living, discipleship in the world. In the context of the city, Christian spirituality entails practices of attentiveness, resistance, reconciliation, and "public-social discernment." This does not mean that occasional retreat from the city is not valuable; as the urban pastors attested, change of place and time at the mountaintop and in the wilderness can be quite renewing. However, it is not *necessary* to withdraw from the urban context; the everyday of city life can be one's primary spiritual habitat. Sheldrake rejects the idea that contemplation somehow redeems action and makes it holy, or that action alone embodies faith. Rather, following the Ignatian insight that God can be found and served "in all things," everyday life in the city itself becomes a series of spiritual exercises, a contemplative public engagement.[18]

All this affirms that the city can indeed be a place of divine disclosure, but how we come to the city—with what stories, habits, practices, rhythms, and friendships—makes all the difference. Urban places, like other places, can be sacred, but they are made sacred by the way we walk (both literally and metaphorically) in and through them. What is needed here is a balance between "a gospel conviction that Christ has redeemed all places, that he is Lord of space and time" and also "the importance of the incarnation in inviting us to value place."[19] What is also needed, we might say, is a balance between understanding the particular way the city is capable of sacramentally rooting us and shaping us in our faith, on the one hand, and the way the experiences, disciplines, and hopes that we bring with us shape our encounter with God in the city, on the other hand. Place, we might say, is not a dead object or destination. It is a performance. Pastor Gutierrez's insights correspond with the work of philosophers, sociologists, and theologians such as Michel de Certeau, Edward Casey, E. V. Walker, or John Inge, who have spent considerable energy theorizing about place and who attempt to steer just such a course between the importance of place and the way that importance is structured relationally by the humans who dwell in it and move through it. Thus, as Walker says, place is

> a location of experience. It evokes and organises memories, images, feelings, sentiments, meanings, and the work of the imagination. The feelings of a place are indeed the mental projections of individuals, but they come from collective experience and do not happen anywhere else. They belong to the place.[20]

If we can affirm, then, that the city is a place where God is active and where God meets us, a place where our faith can be rooted and where we can be reminded of God's presence, the city is also a place that can be redeemed and transformed, a place where we find ourselves empowered by grace to respond so that we do not leave the city the way we found it. The city can be a sacred place because, as a site of incredible diversity, it is the place where we encounter the other. Given the fact that the cities have increasingly become literally reservations of the underclass, the city is also the place where we may encounter Christ in the form of those who lack food, clothing, job skills, or shelter.[21] But to experience the city as sacred place or to encounter God in the city is to be transformed by that encounter so that we do not merely encounter the other in sterile terms nor do we merely look upon those who lack food, clothing, or shelter in voyeuristic terms. To encounter the city sacramentally is to be changed by grace, to be a new and transformed presence in the city.

PILGRIMAGE AND THE CITY

If the city is not intrinsically holy but is so by virtue of what happens there, our relationship to the city is one of commitment and connection but also one of detachment (understood with Brown Taylor as the opposite of attachment—in other words "non-attachment"). This duality is echoed in Augustine's vision of the church as the pilgrim City of God. Augustine began writing *City of God* in 413, just a few years after the invasion of Rome, which would ultimately lead to the collapse of the Roman Empire. Though he employs the word "city" largely as a metaphor within his comprehensive theological framing of history and of the nature of the church in the world, there can be no question that the actual circumstances of Rome and of his and his fellow Christians' relationship to Rome provide the backdrop to this magnificent treatise, one that helps us think about our relationship to the city in terms of pilgrimage and in what sense the earthly city both does and does not serve as a place for our faith.

For Augustine, there are two cities, "the earthly and the Heavenly, which are mingled together from the beginning to the end of their history."[22] The earthly is temporal and estranged from God while the heavenly is eternal and the object of our hope. The church is that part of the heavenly city "which is on pilgrimage in this condition of mortality, and which lives on the basis of faith"; indeed, Augustine can even refer to the church's pilgrimage as "a life of captivity in this earthly city as in a foreign land."[23]

Augustine traces the conflict between the earthly and heavenly cities to Cain and Abel, the sons of Adam and Eve. The

earthly city finds its origin in Cain, who murdered Abel and
built the first city, named Enoch (Gen. 4), after his son; Cain
was concerned with his own finite, temporal existence. Abel, on
the other hand, lived in dependence upon God and "was a pilgrim and stranger in the world, belonging as he did to the City
of God."[24] Augustine's attention to the fratricide that stands
behind the invention of the first city is employed as a parallel
to the fratricide that, as legend has it, stands behind the found-
ing of Rome (Romulus kills Remus), thus contrasting the
earthly city, which is founded upon violence, with the heavenly
city, which is a city of peace. Ultimately, however, Augustine
wants to demonstrate that the two cities are created by two different kinds of love:

> The earthly city was created by self-love reaching the point
> of contempt for God, the Heavenly City by the love of God
> carried as far as contempt of self. In fact, the earthly city
> glories in itself, the Heavenly City glories in the Lord. The
> former looks for glory from men, the latter finds its high-
> est glory in God, the witness of a good conscience. The
> earthly lifts up its head in its own glory, the Heavenly City
> says to its God: "My glory; you lift up my head." In the for-
> mer, the lust for domination lords it over its princes as over
> the nations it subjugates; in the other both those put in
> authority and those subject to them serve one another in
> love, the rulers by their counsel, the subjects by obedience.
> The one city loves its own strength shown in its powerful
> leaders; the other says to its God, "I will love you, my Lord,
> my strength."[25]

As William Cavanaugh points out—and here again there are
resonances to Pastor Gutierrez's insights about the relationship
of sacred time to the experience of the urban context as sacred
place—"The two cities, one formed by the love of God and one
formed by the love of self, occupy not two different spaces but
two different times. The earthly city is not everlasting. Its ends
are perishable, while the heavenly city which sojourns with the
earthly 'shall dwell in the fixed stability of its eternal seat, which

it now with patience waits for.'"[26] This patience, for Augustine, is not passive. In the same way, pastoral ministry in the city is patient not when it is inactive, but when it is no longer marked by an impatience that is evident in our belief that we must always be doing something. Patience is undoubtedly one of the most difficult of Christian virtues to cultivate in modern urban cultures, but essential for sustaining urban pastoral excellence.

Despite what might seem like a rather disparaging view of the earthly city and its rebellion against God in Augustine, it is important to recognize that the heavenly city on pilgrimage and the terrestrial city through which it journeys are intermingled, as with Jesus' parable of the wheat and the tares. In fact, it is impossible for us to know which is which, since "both cities alike enjoy the good things, or are afflicted with the adversities of this temporal state, but with a different faith, a different expectation, a different love, until they are separated by the final judgement, and each receives her own end, of which there is no end."[27] Among those who may appear to be enemies of the City of God "are hidden her future citizens" just as "while the City of God is on pilgrimage in this world, she has in her midst some who are united with her in participation in the sacraments, but who will not join with her in the eternal destiny of the saints."[28]

Even if Augustine can describe life in the earthly city as a "life of captivity," it can also be good, since creation is good.[29] It is just that the peace of the earthly city is always fragmentary and partial, since it is not aimed at the highest good, God's peace. The job of the church ("the Heavenly City in her pilgrimage here on earth") is to defend, seek, and make use of whatever earthly peace is possible ("without detriment to true religion and piety"), but at the same time to ever direct the earthly peace of the city to God's peace, "which is so truly peaceful that it should be regarded as the only peace deserving the name, at least in respect of the rational creation; for this peace is the perfectly ordered and completely harmonious fellowship in the enjoyment of God, and of each other in God."[30]

Conceiving of the church as being on an urban pilgrimage, in other words, means that, without becoming "attached" to the city as our permanent home, we nonetheless actively seek the peace of the city and, indeed, we bear witness to God's distinctive and eternal peace in our own corporate lives together before a watching world. That is, of course, impossible, when we are inappropriately attached to the goods of the city as our highest good, so that our love is disordered and finally we become not pilgrims on a journey to the City of God, but merely tourists.

For urban pastors, the city is not an obstacle on that journey nor is it a mere hoop through which we are asked to jump on our way. It can indeed become a sacred place as the itinerary of our pilgrimage . . . as long as we continue to be reminded that we are on a pilgrimage. It has often been noted that while the Bible begins in a garden, it ends in a city. This heavenly city, however, is a new kind of city where human flourishing and that of the ecosphere take place side by side. The plants and rivers of God's creation are located within the city and central to it instead of being located outside of it as something to which we might flee while running from the pandemonium of urban life. In the closing words of the book of Revelation, we get a wonderful vision of this recreated city, the city of peace.

> Then the angel showed me the river of the water of life, bright as crystal, flowing from the throne of God and of the Lamb through the middle of the street of the city. On either side of the river is the tree of life with its twelve kinds of fruit, producing its fruit each month; and the leaves of the tree are for the healing of the nations. Nothing accursed will be found there any more. But the throne of God and of the Lamb will be in it, and his servants will worship him; they will see his face, and his name will be on their foreheads. And there will be no more night; they need no light of lamp or sun, for the Lord God will be their light, and they will reign forever and ever. (22:1–5)

Conclusion

If the church is to take the city seriously as sacred space, it must have leaders who not only love the city and its people but also have learned the knowledge, skills, and virtues necessary for urban ministry. They have to know how to read and interpret contexts as well as texts, for both may be revelatory of God. They need to know how to cultivate holy friendships and build partnerships across diversity. Urban pastoral leaders have the courage to speak prophetically and the know-how to work for social change. In the midst of their work, they embody a Sabbath spirituality that points others toward the Source of renewal. How do these leaders emerge?

While they may arise out of local urban communities and come with natural gifts for ministry, they are shaped by theological education. It is the task of the seminary—in partnership with congregations—to educate and form leaders for the church. We would argue, in light of our research with urban pastors, that theological education needs to be transformed if we are to send out and sustain excellent urban pastors.

Some of the most powerful encounters we witnessed involved urban pastors and our Boston University School of

Theology students as the pastors shared with students their own love of ministry in the city and encouraged students to culti-vate—early in their development—Sabbath practices, peer friendships, and attentiveness to their ongoing spiritual growth. At research forums with faculty and students, in Pastoral and Spiritual Formation groups, pastors shared their love of urban ministry, their clear sense of vocation, their devotion to the Lord. They also revealed their vulnerabilities, their need for renewal, their failures in caring for family and self. They broke into song and launched into sermons; they spoke openly with the conviction of long experience. They reflected on their own time in seminary and the ways that seminary prepared them—or did not prepare them—for the reality of ministry in the city.

The fervor and authenticity of these pastors was striking. So too were their descriptions of their phenomenal ministries and their open acknowledgments of exhaustion, spiritual dryness, loneliness, and trauma. Could these pastors be dismissed eas-ily—on to the next round of classes, lectures, meetings, papers? Something nagged. Our own rhythms as a seminary seemed out of synch with the rhythms we had invited these pastors to live into . . . balance of work and rest, community and solitude, giv-ing and self-care. And this seemed to be a problem widespread in theological education. Too often, the demands of seminary training reinforce in students from the outset a lopsided mode of ministry that values busyness over rest, effectiveness over fidelity, and accomplishment over relationships. Moreover, given our clear conviction about the importance of place, it became apparent that we needed to go even further in contex-tualizing our curriculum and pedagogy. How could our teach-ing better form students for the urban pastorate?

Urban pastors indicate that their seminary education—divided into traditional areas such as pastoral care, liturgy, and preaching—did not reflect the more wholistic ministry that the city demands. The artificiality of the guilds has to be unlearned in the course of urban ministry, where, for example, pastoral care may well incorporate community organizing, and preach-ing requires skills in social and ethical analysis. To move toward

a more integrated approach to theological education will be difficult, of course, as it requires restructuring of long-standing
organizational principles and retraining of faculty. It is clear to
us, though, that theological education requires more integration of disciplines with attention to the actual practice and context of ministry. Furthermore, students need training in how to
read the context of the city—how to understand demographic
shifts, the dynamics of multicultural communities, the avail-
ability of educational and social services, and the interplay of
political, economic, and social forces in urban life.

Seminaries prepare ministers to serve in a variety of contexts—
urban, rural, and suburban. Thus, we are not advocating that theological education adopt a singular focus on the city. However,
the formation of pastors who can lead the church in the city does
require attention to the distinctive characteristics of urban life
and the distinctive virtues that constitute and sustain urban pastoral excellence. This requires attention in all seminaries, given
widespread urbanization and the importance of the city. Moreover, for a school of theology such as ours, the contextualization
of theological education means taking our own urban context
seriously. What does it mean to teach theology on a busy avenue
in Boston, interrupted by the sounds of the subway running parallel to our campus, where we walk past homeless people keeping
warm on the grate outside our building? These are the kinds of
questions we are pursuing as a faculty, identifying, for example,
the need for faculty training in urban issues and attention to
urban contexts in classes across the curriculum (and not just in
the "urban ministry" course). It also means thinking creatively
about spiritual formation and field education.

The challenges seem enormous because they are structural,
institutional, and philosophical. They are the product of time-
honored ways of providing theological education that divorce
church from academy, define scholarship and theological education solely in terms of a guild orientation toward auxiliary,
nontheological disciplines, and segment spiritual formation as
a special course or set of activities with little or no connection
to the whole of theological education.

The challenges also stem from wider cultural values—particularly noticeable in the city—that emphasize productivity, speed, and activity. Churches and seminaries often take on these values without even noticing. The challenge is to develop a capacity to notice and reflect critically on the cultural values that form all of us, including the ways in which they shape our expectations for education and ministry. This is a shared task for seminary faculty, administrators, staff, students, pastoral leaders, and laity. The cultivation of practices such as Sabbath keeping then happen within that context of critical reflection—practice engendering reflection, reflection leading to transformed practice. Sabbath keeping becomes a countercultural practice that gives a new, life-giving way of being in the midst of a culture that presses us toward dispersion and workaholism. Rather than being another obligation, practices extend a gift, one that does require discipline to receive.

Partnership is key. Here at Boston University School of Theology, we have undertaken several projects to deepen our partnership with pastoral leaders, involving them as partners in the design of courses, in faculty research projects, and as teachers and pastor-scholars in the classroom. The pastoral presence helps to contextualize courses in the life of congregations and naturally brings class discussion to questions of ministry and vocation. The interaction among students, pastors, and faculty is mutually fruitful—students learn from pastors further along in their ministry, pastors benefit from the community and stimulation of the classroom, and faculty research and teaching can be informed by pastoral insights and questions.

Within that context of partnership, then, seminaries and churches can think together about field education. We have come to believe that field education should be situated in congregational teaching sites that not only teach students about urban ministry but explicitly covenant with seminaries to nurture student interns in integrated practices of Sabbath keeping, spiritual renewal, study, and friendship. This means that we need to build congregational ecologies to support the practices of pastoral excellence. The supervising pastor will not be able to mentor students in such practices if she has not grown into them herself. We would strongly recommend, for example, that field education supervisors receive periodic sabbaticals, continuing education opportunities, and time for regular gatherings with a small community of peers (standard clergy associations may not fit the bill here). Yet this is not simply an issue of supporting the pastor. Laity too need experiences of Sabbath rest, opportunities for reading and reflection, experiences of genuine community, and space to discuss the distinctive challenges of the lay vocation. We envision a shared process of formation, then, for laity, pastors, and seminary faculty and students, building a web of relationships as they create an environment of Sabbath space in the city.

We have been continuously challenged by the pastors with whom we are working to think of pastoral excellence not as simply a collection of character traits, competencies, or abilities *possessed* by pastors, but also as a healthy *participation* in particular ecologies of congregation, family, culture, nature, and collegiality. As another way of saying this, to be an excellent pastor is to be supported and prayed for, to be collaborated with and nurtured. In preparing and training pastors, we have to find ways to avoid the externalization and instrumentalization of healthy relationships (reducing them to mere programs) and instead find ways to foster and facilitate them within the educational process. This is extraordinarily difficult when, for example, spiritual formation groups or field education placements are viewed simply as one more requirement in a seminary education or when community worship, spiritual companionship, and self-care are sacrificed in the name of academic or field performance. We are increasingly challenged to find ways to lead our students into the kinds of healthy relationships that we now see as the substance of pastoral excellence for the long haul. When we ask the pastors to report on what makes a pastor "excellent," it is curious that they hardly ever mention any skill set. That is not because pastoral skills are unimportant, but because they are not helpful in a vacuum. Pastoral excellence is learned and sustained in a web of relationships that encourage and model practices of spiritual nurture, Sabbath rest, study and reflection, and friendship.

Practically speaking, there are ways to promote such practices. Congregations together can practice "Church at Rest"— as did some of the urban churches we studied. Seminaries can frame communal worship and other intentional times for prayer and rest as "Sabbath space."[1] Laypersons might experiment with setting aside family Sabbath time and then reflecting about the experience. Adult education forums on Sabbath could be helpful, perhaps led jointly by a scholar in Hebrew Bible or practical theology, a pastor, and a layperson. The training of field education supervisors needs to explicitly address issues of self-care, spiritual renewal, and Sabbath keeping. One field education supervisor, Hyuk Seonwoo, builds into his covenant with students that they each do one hour of self-care (especially exercise) per week. The pastor does Tai Chi, from which he draws language to describe the natural rhythm of creation as "loosen-empty-push." Seonwoo writes: "When we try to float on our backs, we need to loosen and empty ourselves or else we would drown. Backstrokes ("push") require that we loosen and empty first." Structural issues of funding and timing for field education also need to be addressed: how can we enable students to do field education without also holding down a paid job? Should field education be integrated with coursework or done separately in a summer or additional year in a master of divinity program?

As we seek to mentor students in healthy patterns of work, faculty, students, and supervising pastors together can assess the total demands on students. Too often faculty instructors develop their course requirements in isolation, without a clear sense of the cumulative effect on students. More collaborative course design would alleviate some of the pressure points on students and help faculty step out of the guild mentality. Even simple steps, such as putting syllabi side by side to make sure that the collective assignments are paced reasonably throughout the semester, would be helpful. Field education supervisors, too, could help faculty to take into account the increased demand on pastors and students at particular points in the liturgical season so as to avoid, for example, expecting students to prepare for midterms during Holy Week. Again, partnership helps to keep the dual contexts of church and academy clearly in view.

As the School of Theology community interacted with the urban pastors, we noticed that one of the most uncomfortable issues for us was the question of how faculty model balance, self-care, and Sabbath practices in our own lives. One pastor posed this challenging question: "Would a covenant among faculty members regarding their own Sabbath living help to ensure that we model for the students what we are asking of them?" The faculty member who called herself "a dreadful example" was not alone. Indeed, faculty members, too, are formed in particular contexts—including the academic context that emphasizes rigor, accountability to one's guild, productivity (e.g., "publish or perish"), and rhythms of advancement that may jar with the demands of concurrent life stages (e.g., tenure clock competing with biological clock, work competing with family). What notions of time and balance, friendship and self-care result? How then do faculty model practices of pastoral excellence to their students? Like students, faculty need invitations to practices of Sabbath keeping, safe peer community, and spiritual nurture.

Some faculty were distressed that urban pastors did not gravitate more to study and that some pastors perceived a tension between study and Sabbath. Theology professor Shelly Rambo commented: "It concerns me that I—we—may not be training students to *dive into* theological reflection. Are we, in seminary, scaring students away from this kind of reflection instead of igniting their passion for it? The gathering around the study questions should not only be an opportunity to support each other but, at its best, to begin to develop a working theological vision for their communities within the city." Professor of worship Karen Westerfield noted that "theology students should be equipped for a lifetime of combining 'the love of learning and the desire for God' (to use a phrase of Jean Leclercq) for the purpose of service in the world."

Spiritual formation in seminary is best understood as integral to study—not as a distraction from it or as the "real" part of ministry formation with classes seen as disconnected hoops to be jumped through. Study itself can be a spiritual practice—a process of cultivating attentiveness, struggling to understand, engaging the other, seeking knowledge of God. Drawing out the formative aspect of theological study is something that can be done in every seminary course. Moreover, courses can attend to particular links between the subject matter and the life of faith—exploring practices such as worship, prayer, building of community, interpretation of texts, justice, discernment, and ministry. In a university-based school of theology such as ours, one of the major challenges is the diversity of vocations of our students. Classes include both master of divinity and master of theological studies students, for example; not all students are preparing for ministry, and some seek only academic preparation. Still, theological education is inherently spiritual and, while debates about the nature of that spirituality are to be welcomed, theology and spirituality are disconnected only to the detriment of both.

Pastors, early on as ministerial students, need to develop the habits, practices, rhythms, and relationships integral to pastoral excellence, or else they may never develop them at all. Unfortunately, the seminary experience often fails to model and reinforce them and, in fact, models a way of life that is likely to lead to burnout, dysfunction, and a diminished sense of joy and vocation in pastoral ministry. Frequently students suspend spiritual practices that had been important to them when they entered seminary, or postpone developing spiritual disciplines, until they are out of school because they are "too busy." Our work with urban pastors convinces us that the busyness of seminary mirrors the busyness of ministry. How students learn to navigate that pace of life now forms habits that they carry into ministry later. This is relevant to all contexts of ministry, but particular attention needs to be given to the extremely rapid pace of urban life and the disconnect between natural rhythms and the urban sense of time. Thus, spiritual formation has to be understood as formation in the midst of the everyday: formation that is contextualized, organic, critical, and attentive to the presence of God "in all things." The traditions of Jewish and Christian spirituality offer wisdom about divine rhythms, prayerful structuring of time, balance, self-care, and discernment. Inviting students to wrestle with these traditions in the context of their own, immediate life contexts, including the context of urban living, may not resolve the tensions of spiritual formation amid busyness but it will give them practice in the same spiritual work they will continue when they are "out there" in ministry.

Theological education, in short, can create space and develop the art of critical reflection on cultural values, study and conversation with the tradition, and the intentional cultivation of practices of pastoral excellence. Rather than reinforcing unhealthy and unbiblical patterns of overwork and self-neglect, seminaries would form persons who hear the liberating call to dignified work and to rest, to creativity and to awe, to play and to study. This will entail authentic partnership between church and academy. Our vision for theological education entails creating ecologies that support pastoral excellence in the city, nurturing practices of holy friendship, study, Sabbath keeping, and continual re-creation in the spirit.

Notes

Introduction

1. Robert Linthicum, *Empowering the Poor* (Monrovia, CA: MARC Publications, 1991), 21–24.

Chapter 1: Urban Challenge and Opportunity

1. "Mayday 23: World Population Becomes More Urban than Rural," North Carolina State University News Release (May 22, 2007). On May 23, say researchers from North Carolina and Georgia, "a predicted global urban population of 3,303,992,253 will exceed that of 3,303,866,404 rural people."

2. "The world goes to town," *The Economist* (May 3, 2007), http://www.economist.com/surveys/displayStory.cfm?story_id=9 070726.

3. Ibid. Not every state in the United States has a majority of urban dwellers. Some states—Maine, Mississippi, Vermont, and West Virginia—are still predominantly rural.

4. "Issues at the Rural Urban Fringe: The Land Use Debate—Situational Background," EDIS document FE551, published by the Department of Food and Resource Economics, Florida Cooperative Extension Service, Institute of Food and Agricultural Sciences, University of Florida, Gainesville, FL (May 2005), http://edis.ifas.ufl.edu.

5. Robert V. Kemper, "Theological Education for Urban Ministry: A Survey of U.S. Seminaries," *Theological Education* 34:1 (1997): 51–72.

6. Ronald Peters has helpfully suggested that "urban areas are typically defined in one of three ways: *spatially* (in terms of the uniqueness of geography and/or environmental characteristics), *socially* (identifying realities that shape the context and caliber of social interactions: population demographics, and so on), or *symbolically* (referring to the ethos or metaphorical meaning assigned to the metropolis based upon its perceived or projected characteristics, for example, "the Big Apple" or "the

Holy City"). *Urban Ministry: An Introduction* (Nashville: Abingdon Press, 2007), 26.

7. See Michel de Certeau, *The Practice of Everyday Life* (Berkeley: University of California Press, 1984), 117.

8. See Lyle E. Schaller, ed., *Center City Churches: The New Urban Frontier* (Nashville: Abingdon Press, 1993), 14.

9. Michael O. Emerson with Rodney M. Woo, *People of the Dream: Multiracial Congregations in the United States* (Princeton, NJ: Princeton University Press, 2006), 7. Based on the study by Ram Cnaan, et al., *The Invisible Caring Hand: American Congregations and the Provision of Welfare* (New York: New York University Press, 2002).

10. Letty Russell, "The City as Battered Woman," in *Envisioning the New City: A Reader on Urban Ministry*, ed. Eleanor Scott Meyers (Louisville, KY: Westminster/John Knox Press, 1992), 152.

11. Ibid.

12. Dorothy Day described works of mercy as "feeding the hungry, giving drink to the thirsty, clothing the naked, sheltering the homeless, visiting the sick, ransoming the prisoner, and burying the dead." The "spiritual works of mercy," so she says, are "instructing the ignorant, counseling the doubtful, rebuking the sinner, bearing wrongs patiently, forgiving all injuries, and praying for the living and the dead." *Loaves and Fishes* (Maryknoll, NY: Orbis Books, 1963), xvii.

13. Paolo Freire, *Pedagogy of the Oppressed* (New York: Continuum, 1983), 29.

14. Hannah Arendt, *On Revolution* (New York: Viking Press, 1967), 56.

15. Peters, *Urban Ministry*, 33.

16. Michael Emerson, who has produced what could well be considered the definitive study on multiracial congregations (*People of the Dream*), estimates that less than 7 percent of all U.S. congregations are multiracial (no one racial group constituting more than 80 percent of the total membership). Protestants, who constitute 84 percent of all congregations nationwide, are even more segregated than the whole, with only 5 percent of their congregations being multiracial. About 15 percent of all Roman Catholic congregations are multiracial, though Roman Catholic congregations make up only 7 percent of the total. Public schools are six times more racially diverse than religious congregations. Emerson and Woo, *People of the Dream*, 36–39.

17. U.S. Bureau of the Census, *The Foreign-Born Population in the United States, 2003* (August 2004), 1.

18. U.S. Bureau of the Census, *2003 American Community Survey.* Other notable cities are Boston (30 percent), Houston (27 percent), Dallas (26 percent), San Diego (25 percent), and Chicago (22 percent).

19. Friere, *Pedagogy*, 137.

20. Peters, *Urban Ministry*, 15.

21. See Donna Schaper, "Bricks without Straw: Ministry in the City," in Meyers, *Envisioning the New City*, 31.

22. Schaller, *Center City Churches*, 179.

23. Jackson Carroll, *God's Potters: Pastoral Leadership and the Shaping of Congregations* (Grand Rapids: Eerdmans, 2006), 113–14.

24. John P. Kretzmann and John L. McKnight, *Building Communities from Inside Out: A Path toward Finding and Mobilizing a Community's Assets* (Evanston, IL: Northwestern University, 1993), 1.

25. Ibid., 5.

26. Ibid.

27. Ibid.

Chapter 2: Cultivating Holy Friendships

1. Aristotle, *Nichomachean Ethics*, trans. Terence Irwin (Indianapolis: Hackett Publishing Company, 1999), VIII:1, 119.

2. Howard Thurman, *Jesus and the Disinherited* (Boston: Beacon Press), 75.

3. The Pulpit and Pew project of Duke Divinity School conducts research aimed at strengthening the quality of pastoral leadership (clergy and lay) in churches, parishes, and other faith communitites across the United States.

4. Carroll, *God's Potters*, 179–80.

5. Ibid., 176–77.

6. Cited in Stanley Hauerwas, *The Peaceable Kingdom: A Primer in Christian Ethics* (Notre Dame, IN: University of Notre Dame Press, 1983), 151. Cf. David Burrell, "Contemplation and Action: Personal Spirituality/World Reality," in *Dimensions of Contemporary Spirituality*, ed. Francis A. Eigo, OSA (Philadelphia: Villanova University Press, 1982), 152.

7. Paul J. Wadell, *Becoming Friends* (Grand Rapids: Brazos Press, 2002), 45.

8. L. Gregory Jones and Kevin R. Armstrong, *Resurrecting Excellence: Shaping Faithful Christian Ministry* (Grand Rapids: Eerdmans, 2006), 65.

9. Wadell, *Becoming Friends*, 17.

10. Jones and Armstrong, *Resurrecting Excellence*, 65.

11. Ibid.

12. Augustine, *The Confessions of St. Augustine*, trans. Rex Warner (New York: New American Library, 1963), IV:4, 73.

13. Ibid., 78.

14. Jones and Armstrong, *Resurrecting Excellence*, 68.

15. It may be worth noting at this point that four seemed to be the perfect number for these partnerships. Those with whom we consulted who are skilled in small-group process suggest that three-person groups are too small for authentic community because they create an opportunity for one person to be left out while two members bond, while the number five begins to move the group beyond an ability to foster intimate dialogue.

16. Wadell, *Becoming Friends*, 56.

17. Ibid., 42.

18. Ibid., 50.

19. Aristotle, *Nichomachean Ethics*, VIII.3, 121.

20. Ibid., 122.

21. Stanley Hauerwas and Charles Pinches, *Christians among the Virtues: Theological Conversations with Ancient and Modern Ethics* (Notre Dame, IN: University of Notre Dame Press, 1997), 38.

Chapter 3: Sabbath Practices

1. See, e.g., Tamara C. Eskenazi, Daniel J. Harrington, SJ, and William H. Shea, eds., *The Sabbath in Jewish and Christian Traditions* (New York: Crossroad, 1991).

2. Elliot K. Ginsburg, *The Sabbath in Classical Kabbalah* (Albany: State University of New York Press, 1989), 60.

3. Abraham Joshua Heschel, *The Sabbath* (New York: Farrar, Straus, and Giroux, 1951), 29.

4. Scholars debate interpretations of such texts, as to whether they do away with the Sabbath command for followers of Jesus Christ or whether they continue to express the real meaning of the Sabbath. On this point, see, e.g., Eskenazi, Harrington, and Shea, *Sabbath in Jewish and Christian Traditions*.

5. Heschel, *Sabbath*, 30.

6. Wendell Berry, *A Timbered Choir: The Sabbath Poems 1979–1997* (Washington, DC: Counterpoint, 1998), 5.

7. Douglas Burton-Christie, "Solitude, the Ground of Compassion," *Journal of Supervision and Training in Ministry* 18 (1997): 130–31.

8. Heschel, *Sabbath*, 32.

9. Art Ritter, sermon titled "Sacred Time," First Congregational Church, Salt Lake City, Utah. Reverend Ritter notes that the story is not original and that a version of it appears in Stephen R. Covey, *The Seven Habits of Highly Effective People: Powerful Lessons in Personal Change* (New York: Simon and Schuster, 1989), 287.

10. Heschel, *Sabbath*, 14.

11. Aryeh Kaplan, *Sabbath Day of Eternity* (New York: National Conference of Synagogue Youth, 1974), 19.

12. On this point, see, e.g., Craig Dykstra, "Reconceiving Practice," in *Shifting Boundaries: Contextual Approaches to the Structure of Theological Education*, ed. Barbara G. Wheeler and Edward Farley (Louisville, KY: Westminster/John Knox Press, 1991), 45.

13. Dorothy C. Bass, "Christian Formation for Sabbath Rest," *Interpretation* 59:1 (2006): 36.

Chapter 4: Renewing the Spirit

1. Thomas Merton, trans., *The Wisdom of the Desert: Sayings from the Desert Fathers of the Fourth Century* (New York: New Directions Publishing Company, 1970), 55, 30, 74, 73–74.

2. See chap. 6 in Timothy Fry, OSB, trans., *Rule of Saint Benedict in English* (Collegeville, MN: Liturgical Press, 1980).

3. Caroline Stephen, excerpt from *Quaker Strongholds*, in *Quaker Spirituality: Selected Writings*, ed. Douglas V. Steere (New York: Paulist Press, 1984), 250.

4. For discussion of the value of silence that includes reflection on the Sinai and Elijah experiences, see "The Value of Silence," http://www.taize.fr/en_article12.html.

5. Fry, *Rule of Saint Benedict*, chap. 43.

6. Lewis Nicholson, "Sabbath and Social Monasticism: Spending Time in the Presence of God," keynote address, Sustaining Urban Pastoral Excellence Concluding Conference, Boston University, October 10, 2007.

7. Stephanie Paulsell, "Honoring the Body," in *Practicing Our Faith*, ed. Dorothy C. Bass (San Francisco: Jossey-Bass, 1998), 14.

8. Ibid., 6.

Chapter 5: Finding God in the City

1. Barbara Brown Taylor, "Looking for God in the City: A Meditation," in Meyers, *Envisioning the New City*, 183.

2. John Inge, *A Christian Theology of Place* (Aldershot: Ashgate Publishing, 2003), 14.

3. On the genealogy of this shift, see ibid., 5ff.

4. Harvey Cox, *The Secular City: Secularization and Urbanization in Theological Perspective* (New York: Macmillan, 1965).

5. Belden Lane, *The Solace of Fierce Landscapes: Exploring Desert and Mountain Spirituality* (Oxford: Oxford University Press, 1998), 10. See also Edward Farley, *Theologia: The Fragmentation and Unity of Theological Education* (Philadelphia: Fortress Press, 1983), who describes *habitus* as the "habit of the human soul" (31) or "aptitude of the soul" (36). Farley laments the loss of *theologia* as *habitus*.

6. Richard Rogers, *Cities for a Small Planet* (London: Faber and Faber, 1997), quoted in Inge, *Christian Theology of Place*, 19.

7. Ibid., 19–20.

8. Ibid., 20.

9. See Inge, *Christian Theology of Place*, 7–11.

10. Ibid.

11. Ibid., 81.

12. Brown Taylor, "Looking for God," 184.

13. Ibid.

14. Ibid., 184–85.

15. Ibid., 185.

16. Ibid., 187.

17. Philip F. Sheldrake, "Christian Spirituality as a Way of Living Publicly: A Dialectic of the Mystical and the Prophetic," in *Minding the Spirit: The Study of Christian Spirituality*, ed. Elizabeth A. Dreyer and Mark S. Burrows (Baltimore: Johns Hopkins University Press, 2005), 282–98. The reference to Ignatius comes from the "Contemplation to Attain Love" in week four of his *Spiritual Exercises*. See George E. Ganss, SJ, ed., *Ignatius of Loyola: The Spiritual Exercises and Selected Works* (New York: Paulist Press, 1991), 176.

18. Ibid.

19. Inge, *Christian Theology of Place*, 58.

20. Quoted in ibid., 83.

21. Eighty-eight percent of the poor are urban in the Northeast, 85 percent in the West, 70 percent in the Midwest, and 66 percent in the

South. Randall Bartlett, *The Crisis of America's Cities* (Armonk, NY: M. E. Sharpe, 1998), 7.

22. Augustine, *Concerning the City of God against the Pagans*, trans. Henry Bettenson (New York: Penguin Books, 1984), XVIII.54

23. Ibid., XIX.17.

24. Ibid., XV.1.

25. Ibid., XIV.28.

26. William Cavanaugh, *Torture and Eucharist: Theology, Politics, and the Body of Christ* (Oxford: Blackwell, 1998), 215.

27. Augustine, *Concerning the City of God*, XVIII.54.

28. Ibid., I.35.

29. Tripp York, *The Purple Crown: The Politics of Martyrdom* (Scottdale, PA: Herald Press, 2007), 102.

30. Augustine, *Concerning the City of God*, XIX.17.

Conclusion

1. Doctoral student Susan Forshey has introduced a weekly "Sabbath Space" into the School of Theology. Worship leaders at the school also drew connections between Sabbath and communal worship.

Bibliography

Arendt, Hannah. *On Revolution.* New York: Viking Press, 1967.

Aristotle. *Nichomachean Ethics.* Translated by Terence Irwin. Indianapolis: Hackett Publishing Company, 1999.

Augustine. *Concerning the City of God against the Pagans.* Translated by Henry Bettenson. New York: Penguin Books, 1984.

———. *The Confessions of St. Augustine.* Translated by Rex Warner. New York: New American Library, 1963.

Bartlett, Randall. *The Crisis of America's Cities.* Armonk, NY: M. E. Sharpe, 1998.

Bass, Dorothy C. "Christian Formation for Sabbath Rest." *Interpretation* 59:1 (2006).

———, ed. *Practicing Our Faith.* San Francisco: Jossey-Bass, 1998.

Berry, Wendell. *A Timbered Choir: The Sabbath Poems 1979–1997.* Washington, DC: Counterpoint, 1998.

Burton-Christie, Douglas. "Solitude, the Ground of Compassion." *Journal of Supervision and Training in Ministry* 18 (1997).

Carroll, Jackson W. *God's Potters: Pastoral Leadership and the Shaping of Congregations.* Grand Rapids: Eerdmans, 2006.

Cavanaugh, William. *Torture and Eucharist: Theology, Politics, and the Body of Christ.* Oxford: Blackwell, 1998.

Cox, Harvey. *The Secular City: Secularization and Urbanization in Theological Perspective.* New York: Macmillan, 1965.

Day, Dorothy. *Loaves and Fishes.* Maryknoll, NY: Orbis Books, 1963.

Dreyer, Elizabeth A., and Mark S. Burrows, eds. *Minding the Spirit: The Study of Christian Spirituality.* Baltimore: Johns Hopkins University Press, 1985.

Emerson, Michael O., with Rodney M. Woo. *People of the Dream: Multiracial Congregations in the United States.* Princeton, NJ: Princeton University Press, 2006.

Eskenazi, Tamara C., Daniel J. Harrington, SJ, and William H. Shea, eds. *The Sabbath in Jewish and Christian Traditions.* New York: Crossroad, 1991.

Freire, Paulo. *Pedagogy of the Oppressed*. New York: Continuum, 1983.

Fry, Timothy, OSB, trans. *Rule of Saint Benedict in English*. Collegeville, MN: Liturgical Press, 1980.

Ganss, George, SJ, ed. *Ignatius of Loyola: The Spiritual Exercises and Selected Works*. New York: Paulist Press, 1991.

Ginsburg, Elliot K. *The Sabbath in Classical Kabbalah*. Albany: State University of New York Press, 1989.

Hauerwas, Stanley. *The Peaceable Kingdom: A Primer in Christian Ethics*. Notre Dame, IN: University of Notre Dame Press, 1983.

Hauerwas, Stanley, and Charles Pinches. *Christians among the Virtues: Theological Conversations with Ancient and Modern Ethics*. Notre Dame, IN: University of Notre Dame Press, 1997.

Heschel, Abraham Joshua. *The Sabbath*. New York: Farrar, Straus, and Giroux, 1951.

Inge, John. *A Christian Theology of Place*. Aldershot: Ashgate Publishing, 2003.

Jones, L. Gregory, and Kevin R. Armstrong. *Resurrecting Excellence: Shaping Faithful Christian Ministry*. Grand Rapids: Eerdmans, 2006.

Kaplan, Aryeh. *Sabbath Day of Eternity*. New York: National Conference of Synagogue Youth, 1974.

Kretzmann, John P., and John L. McKnight. *Building Communities from Inside Out: A Path toward Finding and Mobilizing a Community's Assets*. Evanston, IL: Northwestern University, 1993.

Lane, Belden. *The Solace of Fierce Landscapes: Exploring Desert and Mountain Spirituality*. Oxford: Oxford University Press, 1998.

Linthicum, Robert. *Empowering the Poor*. Monrovia, CA: World Vision, 1991.

Merton, Thomas, trans. *The Wisdom of the Desert: Sayings from the Desert Fathers of the Fourth Century*. New York: New Directions Publishing Company, 1970.

Meyers, Eleanor Scott, ed. *Envisioning the New City: A Reader on Urban Ministry*. Louisville, KY: Westminster/John Knox Press, 1992.

Paulsell, Stephanie. *Honoring the Body: Meditations on a Christian Practice*. San Francisco: Jossey-Bass, 2003.

Peters, Ronald E. *Urban Ministry: An Introduction*. Nashville: Abingdon Press, 2007.

Schaller, Lyle E. *Center City Churches: The New Urban Frontier*. Nashville: Abingdon Press, 1993.